Haven Network,

I hope this i
motivator for c

Enjoy,

Lisa Cybaniak
lisacybaniak@lifelikeyoumeanit.com

Survivor to Warrior

YOU have the power
to change your life!

By

Lisa Cybaniak

Self-Development

First Printed in United Kingdom 2019

Published by Conscious Dreams Publishing
www.consciousdreamspublishing.com

Editor: Lee Dickinson
www.wordwisewebltd.com

Cover Design: Jae Thompson
www.cvajae.com

Typeset: Nadia Vitushynska

ISBN: 978-1-912551-62-0

Dedication

For my Mum, who has never once doubted me.
Her complete belief in me literally saved my life.

In this book, you will learn:

- Powerful techniques to reframe limiting and outdated belief systems holding you back
- Transformational ways to rewrite your script and become your own hero
- How to use positive intentions and affirmations to increase self-confidence
- How to strengthen your connection through meditation and self-reflection
- How the power of forgiveness can transform your life for the better

Contents

• Chapter 1 •

My Story

Trigger Warning

In the 1970s, when I was born, support systems for single mums just did not exist. In fact, when my mum decided to divorce my father, a raging alcoholic, she needed to ask for her father's permission.

With no support from society available, my mum brought me to live with her sister and her four boys. She was 'tainted' with the shame of being a divorcee. For nearly two years, my mum and auntie struggled to make ends meet for the five children.

When my mum met a man 'willing' to date a divorced single mother, she thought she had won the Lottery! I was two years old when my mum and I moved in with him to start living as a family. Being so young, my memories of that time are very vague. I have some pleasant memories of sitting on his shoulders to see above all the people in the park, for example.

While the memory of many of the events is fuzzy, the feeling I had during the first couple of years is crystal clear. I was afraid, angry, and overwhelmed with a feeling of injustice. I loathed this man with every fibre of my being, and the fact that my feelings were brushed aside, assumed to be due to my lack of one-on-one time with my mother, left me seething. I was filled with hatred.

We moved a lot – roughly every two years – so I tend to remember my age during key events based on where we lived at the time. My earliest memories of this man involved the first home we all lived in together, making me between two to four years old. He was annoyed with how slowly I ate my dinner, so began a punishment system to entice me to eat quickly. If I was not able to finish my dinner at the same time as him, he would grab an enormous decorative wooden spoon off the wall and force-feed me with it. If I protested, I got the strap. Over the years, this led to regular beatings with his belt, for various offences – usually things beyond my control given my age.

Eventually he grew bored of my weakness and began training me to fight, so I would be more of a challenge. He forced me to watch boxing matches and then would spend hours breaking down the moves with me, teaching me to punch and block. While that may sound like a great stepfather daughter moment, it was not. He rarely held back with his punches, sending me flying into walls, down stairs, and against hard furniture. If I cried, he would say, 'I will give you something to cry about'. And he was a man of his word.

By the time I was seven I could defend myself well, and by nine I could inflict enough pain to cause him to flinch. That is when his abuse took a devastating turn, physically and sexually.

Physically, his punishments began to get more sinister. I wore clips in my hair that my mother made. I loved the clips, but had no choice in wearing them. If my hair fell into my eyes, I would be beaten. So, my 'look' became one of hair clips, every day, except for when I wore a headband. One day, while sitting in an assembly at school, it felt like one clip was slipping. When I went to remove it to fasten it again more securely, it broke in my hand. I was beside myself. I knew he would never believe me and I would pay a hefty price.

Sure enough, when I got home from school, after trying desperately to use my one remaining hair clip to hold up all the hair, I found him in the front porch talking with the neighbour's grown son. He did his usual – keeping a calm face, he greeted me kindly with 'School was good then, Lisa?'. His eyes told a story I knew too well. Deep behind his open kindness was a sense of pleasure for what was to come. Perhaps even a pleasure for deceiving the neighbour's son. He asked me what happened to my hair clip and I told him, with as much courage as I could muster. Again, because of the presence of someone else, he brushed it off, pretending it did not matter and I had problem-solved well.

When the neighbour left, my stepfather told me to wait in the porch. I heard him turn on the tap in the kitchen. He returned, picked me up, whipped off my school bag, lifted my shirt and jacket, and forcibly held me in the kitchen sink, the hot water from the tap running down the bare skin of my back.

Then there was a time I was doing dishes. He told me to be careful as there was a lot of glass to clean. I fumbled and a broke a glass. The next thing I knew, I was pinned to the ground, with him on top of me, using his knees to pin my arms down, sitting on my chest. He had a piece of the broken glass in his hand and used it to cut open the back of my left hand for being so clumsy, and the backs of both ears for not listening to him. These are just a taste of the memories of physical abuse left in my memory banks.

I became fully aware of the sexual abuse when I was nine. Like most children, I was a very sound sleeper. I woke up one evening, when I was roughly nine, to find him kneeling at my bedside, a flashlight in hand, and my pyjamas and underwear around my ankles. Instantly, I knew that if I showed him I was awake, I would not survive the night. I pretended to still be asleep and did my best impression of what I thought it would look like to begin waking from a sleeping state. It worked. He quickly re-dressed me and left the room.

I have no way of knowing if that was truly the first time, or just the first time I awoke. There would be countless more episodes as the next couple of years unfolded. I tried everything I could to prevent it. I had a large King-sized bed and would wrap myself up like a sausage roll with my duvet, and sleep in the centre of the bed. I thought the act of him needing to roll me over to the side, and unroll me from the duvet would awaken me before he began assaulting me. Nope. I do not know how he did it, but every time I woke up, I would be over on the side of the bed, and already unwrapped from the duvet.

However, I was able to piece together one bit. A few times I woke up to find I was still fully dressed, and he was lightly tickling my feet. I would still pretend to just stir, rather than sitting right up, for fear of his reaction. So, that was partly how he pulled it off – if I awoke to having my feet tickled, he left; if not then he stayed.

I am not entirely sure when the psychological abuse began. I do not remember the first occasion. What I do remember is always being told flat out that I was ugly, stupid, worthless, and useless. He would add in how nobody was ever going to love me and I would never amount to anything in life.

He also started a nickname for me, which must have begun when I was only a few years old, because I do not remember a starting point – it was always my nickname: Gonzo. You know, after the Sesame Street character with the enormous nose? No, I did not have a large nose. It was just another way to bring me down and crush my self-esteem so that I would honestly believe I did not deserve better. And it worked.

From what I understand, it is exactly the same as domestic violence cases – where the abuser first works on the psyche of their victim, ensuring the victim is in a state of pure self-loathing before they escalate their offences, as their way of controlling and manipulating the victim, but also to ensure the victim never speaks up and leaves.

This was what he was doing to my mother, from the beginning. He was smart enough to know that abusing the daughter of an empowered woman would land him in jail. So, he took his time to diminish her self-confidence as well. He did not have to wait very long, as my mother was already vulnerable then, due to the isolation and judgement she felt from society as a single, divorced mum.

It did not help that no soul ever stepped forward to help. I have a strong memory of being eight years old, sleeping in my bed when they returned home from a night out with friends. The other couple had come in for a nightcap and an argument started between him and my mother. He began strangling her. I could hear her gasped cries for help, her desperate struggle to get him off her. I could also hear the other man very calmly telling him to forget about it, it was not worth it, and asking for another drink. While I, an eight-year-old child, was steeling myself to run out to confront this monster and save my mother, this adult was just standing there, calmly reassuring him it was not worth it – that *she* was not worth it.

These types of experiences do something to us. They leave a mark so deep we lose sight of its very existence, while it silently affects every fibre of our being. It was not that the man did not physically jump in to save my mother. Heck, his calm demeanour may have been exactly what saved her. The fact he and his wife stayed and had a few more drinks is what spoke volumes to me. It said, loud and clear, his actions were acceptable, and no one was going to save us.

If you know anyone who has been in a domestic violence situation, you know what it does to their confidence and sense of self-worth. My mother was no exception. While he did most of his abuse behind closed doors – certainly the sexual abuse, but even most of the physical attacks – the abuse she would have witnessed would have been explained away immediately. Not because he was such a good liar, but because she was in a place of feeling this was her only chance. By then, she already felt like nobody else would or *could* love her. That was his plan, and it worked.

On the other hand, I was doing something similar. I knew everything going on in my home was wrong, and definitely not normal. I also thought all the adults in my life knew what was happening, even my mother. As a child, adults were super-heroes. They had all the answers, even long before the internet was available to quickly double check. It did not occur to me they could not know what was happening behind closed doors. I believed everyone knew – from my mother to my friends' parents, to my teachers and other family members – and, like that man, were choosing to do nothing. This caused me to feel like I was not worth saving.

I did attempt to reach out a couple of times. I thought if I wrote it out in a letter, the person reading it would be obligated to do something. So I wrote out what was happening to me and gave it to my friend to take home to her mum. Her mum knew my family as she had looked after me before and after school for a couple years, albeit a few years earlier. My friend read the letter and approached me to ask if it was real. I nodded, and she gave me a hug and said she would show it to her mum. I never heard a word back and my friend began spending less and less time with me. Now that may have been a complete coincidence, but not for my brain. For me, it was directly related to her knowing what was happening. She was judging me and had decided I was not good enough to be her friend.

See how my belief about myself affected my perception of the situation? We would have only been ten or eleven years old. She was probably frightened, and our losing touch may have been completely unrelated. But, in my brain, there was a direct relationship between telling people my story and losing important people in my life.

One day, when I was twelve, a miracle happened. My mum came home from work, sat me down, and asked me point blank if he had been touching me. My first reaction was to say no and act disgusted, I imagine out of shame. Luckily, I stopped myself and instead just nodded.

We spoke briefly about it, with her asking some specific questions and me answering honestly. It was my first realisation she had not known, all those years. I felt so foolish and ashamed for not realising I needed to tell her, that she did not magically know everything.

She reassured me everything was going to be fine. She needed a few days to make some arrangements and then we would leave. She gave me strict instructions to scream as loud as I could and take my bedside light, which was quite substantial, and hit him with it if I awoke to find him at my side again. This would give her time to get into the room and save me. Luckily, it never came to that.

The next day, she had sorted out living arrangements and came home from work and told me to pack a suitcase. She said to take anything I wanted to keep because she did not know if I would see anything else again. We took the dog, our suitcases, and the clothes on our back, packed them all in one car and left everything else behind. My mum was sure he would know she had discovered his secret when he realised we had left. She was even more sure he would do anything to keep me from telling his secret.

She hired a taxi company to take me to school, insisting it be the same driver so I would recognise him. I was instructed to not enter the car if it was not that specific driver. The school was informed and they kept me in at recess and lunch, in case he attempted to kidnap me. I was not allowed to play with my friends after school, for fear of them discovering where I was, or of him finding me at theirs.

It was a tremendously frightening time, but eventually my mum realised that he did not really care – at least, he did not seem to be willing to do anything to track me down or silence me, although I was not talking anyway.

I was taken to therapy so I could talk about the abuse and my feelings. But here is the thing, I had coped wonderfully throughout my abuse by detaching from the situation. It was like I was having an out-of-body experience, with my body experiencing the trauma while I was able to protect my mind. I did not have a connection to my body any more. I was unable to talk about my feelings with a therapist because I was disconnected. To have feelings was bad – punishable even.

There was also the shame. The last thing I wanted was to see the look of pity in people's faces. I did not want *anyone* to know what I went through. I just wanted to be *normal*. I thought, at the tender age of twelve, that if I ignored it, it would go away and I would be like everyone else. What I feared most were the potential questions: 'Why did you not say something?', 'Why did you not leave?', 'Why did you not fight back?' I was asking myself those questions – even more so since discovering the people I thought knew and were not doing anything, actually did not know at all.

The guilt I began to feel was overwhelming. I knew I was not responsible for the abuse itself, but I was feeling like my inaction allowed it to go on for years longer than it needed to. That then increased the shame. Did I secretly enjoy being beaten down this way? At age sixteen I decided, with the help of another counsellor, I was going to tell the police.

My mum had a breakdown right in front of me and my counsellor. She was so frightened for my safety that she did not know how to support me with my need to seek justice while keeping me safe. So, she went out and legally bought a firearm, then registered at a gun club and began target shooting.

We spoke about installing an alarm system in the house, but could not as we were renting. With that not being an option, she went to all the males in the complex we were living in, especially the ones that faced our property, and gave a description of my now ex-stepfather. She gave them enough information for them to realise how serious the situation was, and to be vigilant about keeping their eyes and ears open to anything suspicious.

Then she called the police and our family lawyer. They both gave her the same advice: drop it. Essentially, they said it would be my word against his and I was just a teenager. The fact we had left four years earlier and I was just coming forward now would be scrutinised and would affect my credibility. The police officer my mum spoke to even told her everyone would know – my friends, and even people on the street – because the media would post my name and picture all over the paper. I was a minor, so of course any identifiable information about me was not allowed. But I did not know that at just sixteen. I was naive and scared.

Again, that belief I was not worth saving came back. I thought if the police – the very people who are sworn to protect us – do not think I deserve justice or protection, then I do not. I dropped my intention to file my report, and even dropped the counsellor. I was too ashamed to return to her office and explain why I was defeated – why the man who had devastated my life was still roaming free, devastating the lives of countless others, because I was too weak.

You can imagine what all this did to my already-fragile state. That mantra in my head – his words that I was ugly, stupid, useless, and worthless – became even louder.

One day, early in my twenties, I woke up and asked a really serious question. Why am I attaching so much value to the words and opinion of a man I loathe, would never trust, and do not respect? I began to take a hard look at the deeply-rooted beliefs I had about myself, and realised every one of them were there because of the actions and words of that man. All my experiences until that point were viewed through this self-deprecating lens, choosing to see the truth in his words. I chose to see 'evidence' I was ugly, stupid, worthless, and useless. But was there actually any *real* evidence to support this? Absolutely not!

Slowly, I began to look at every belief and look at the real evidence. Every time, the evidence disproved the belief. I then worked on re-writing my script. Since my abuse defined me and I did not know myself outside of it, I decided to begin my new script with the opposite belief for each. For example, instead of being ugly, I was beautiful; instead of stupid, I was intelligent.

My confidence began to grow, and I began to choose to see these positive beliefs over my past limiting beliefs. This allowed me to add more detail to my script. Instead of just being beautiful, I began to add all the ways I am beautiful. I spoke about my intentions, my goals and aspirations to help others, my kind heart, and my physical appearance. I found my beauty. I did this with each of my beliefs until the thought of playing that old mantra was laughable!

In 2016, I wrote my 'coming out' blog, where I spoke about surviving abuse for the first time. All of my friends and family had no idea. They all came back with messages of support and love.

But one stuck out. One of my longest friends privately responded to my blog post with her own story. It turns out both of us had experienced similar childhoods, and potentially life-threatening consequences. In our teen years we both wanted to end our lives, not because we did not want to live, but because we wanted to end the pain. Neither of us confided in the other during those years, out of shame. We both felt such strong shame, thinking we would lose each other's friendship if the other knew our secret, that we each suffered in silence, sometimes while we were even sitting back-to-back.

The knowledge I could have had someone to talk to that truly understood, and I could have helped another while being helped myself, but did not out of shame, fuelled an anger. I thought, 'enough is enough' and decided my life's mission was to shed the stigma of being abused by breaking my silence.

Immediately I began to write and post more blogs. I also began looking at helping others while reaching that mission through business. Helping others has always been at the root of everything I do. Sometimes it can be selfish, I admit. By helping others, I am forced to help myself, as the only way to truly help is to lead by example.

Fast-forward two-and-a-half years, at the time of writing this book, and I have left my day job to be a full-time Motivational Speaker and NLP Coach, running online coaching programmes and courses for survivors. Building a life of value and worth after abuse is possible – I am living proof! It took hard work, a deep look at my beliefs, an understanding of what I was getting out of keeping my mantra, and a change of perspective on life and my experiences within it.

This was the hardest work I have ever done, and also the most rewarding. I hope the insights found here will set you on a path of healing and growth so you may find your value and worth. You deserve it!

• Chapter 2 •

Meeting Our Needs

Our past experiences have a tremendous effect on our actions and reactions in everyday life. Long after a traumatic event or abusive situation has ended, it impacts every part of our existence. We are constantly in a state of learning, especially when we are children. Everything is new to us. We need to learn how to eat, walk and talk, and what literally everything in the world is. We learn how to kick a ball without falling over, to hold a pencil, to make a bed, to say please and thank you, and how to wash our hands before a meal.

All of these lessons stick with us throughout the rest of our lives. None more so than the greatest lesson we will learn: How to get what we want. That is right! From the moment we are born, we have needs to meet. We cannot meet them ourselves, so we learn very quickly how to get those needs met through others. Depending on the temperament of our parents or carers, we learn how to get attention and feel heard and understood either positively or negatively. And that, in turn, gives us our sense of worth.

When I was a child, my mum would take me grocery shopping without any issue. I have asked her many times if she remembers me having any tantrums or generally being difficult when we were out and about, and the answer is always, 'no'.

We laugh about how perfect I was, but the truth goes far deeper. I had learned how to get my way, and it was NOT by being difficult. As you read earlier, I had an abusive stepfather. I had learned that being difficult caused massive punishment, even aged five. I was able to weigh out my options, and make a choice to go along shopping, sit nicely in the cart, not ask for anything, and generally help my mum, even with him nowhere in sight. I knew that by doing otherwise, the attention I would get at home, and pain it would cause me, was too great. It was not worth the risk.

I had also learned something else – that if I was not difficult, sat nicely in the car, did not ask for anything, and generally helped my mum, she would reward my good behaviour. That is right, I had learned that I did not need to raise a fuss to get attention and a treat. Instead, I needed to toe the line. I never left that shop, or any other like it, without something.

Now, my case may be extreme, but the fact remains that even as babies we are learning how to get our needs met. A baby sitting in a high chair that has developed enough hand-eye coordination to be able to spot her favourite toy, reach out for it, grab it and hold on to it while she admires and plays with it, will then throw it on the floor. She will immediately go into a fit, sobbing over the loss. She feels the pain of losing her favourite thing.

An adult will pick up the toy and hand it back to her. Instantly her little face will light up with pure joy at the return of her favourite thing. You guessed it; within a few seconds, she will throw it back on the floor.

Why? Why would she feel the great pain at the loss of her toy, the pure joy at its return, and then knowingly put herself through the pain again? Because she knows it will be returned. She has experienced both the pain and the joy and has made a choice to feel the joy again. To feel that joy, she must endure the pain. She is willing to do so because she has determined the brief surge of pain is worth the elated feeling of joy.

Of course, for her need to feel joy to be met, she is relying on another human to return her toy. And they will, because a little child is heartbroken. And the adult has also learned something – when they give the child the toy, the child's smile lighting up the room will give them a sense of accomplishment.

And there you have it. This child has now learned how to meet her need to feel pure joy. Now, if she continues to meet this need in this way when she is a twenty-five-year-old, she will have a serious problem.

And herein lies the premise of this book. ***Survivor to Warrior*** is literally referring to how the coping mechanisms and tools we used to meet our needs in the past are not necessarily fit for purpose in the present. We must evolve as we mature. Our core needs will always remain constant. We are always looking to get attention, be heard and understood, accepted and loved. Hand in hand, we are always looking for these needs to be met externally because someone else's ability to give us these things is a reflection of our worth. Thus, if these needs are not met, or if the person we are hoping to meet these needs for us is going about it in a negative way, our perception of our own value and worth diminishes. This causes a vicious cycle whereby our diminished sense of self-worth causes us to surround ourselves with people and situations that reinforce these feelings. In essence, we surround ourselves with people who are unable to meet our needs because we do not believe we deserve to have our needs met in the first place.

It might just blow your mind at this point to realise those people cannot meet your needs right now because they are trying to get their own needs met. AND they may have learned in *their* childhood that the only way to feel good about themselves is to put down everyone around them. You walk into their lives throwing your favourite toy on the ground, screaming in floods of tears, and they do not pick it back up for you. They may even say or do things to make you feel foolish, disrespected, and truly undervalued. You have not had your needs met at all.

Here is the strange part: Most of us will begin to feel an internal pressure now. This is the pressure from our ego telling us that if we can get our needs met by this person, who clearly undervalues and disrespects us, then we will truly be valued and worthy. This is how unhealthy relationships begin and why we prolong our time in them. At the core of it, we are trying to get our needs met, usually using the same tactics we used in childhood that no longer serve us. Moreover, we are relying on someone else to meet those needs. We have lost ourselves in our own egos, in our desire to meet our needs at all costs.

But there is good news: You have the power to change this. You have the power and ability to learn and understand your needs, to develop new ways of meeting those needs, and to develop a true sense of self-value and self-worth. And it all starts here.

As we take this journey together, it may seem like we saunter away from this core truth, but we will always find our way back. At the heart of this book, we are *always* looking at what your needs are and how to meet them in a positive way, by looking within.

• Chapter 3 •

Belief in the Universe

When referring to the Universe, I am talking about the energy all around us. It flows effortlessly, not just around us but through us. It connects us as it *is* us.

Everything on the planet is made of energy, because everything exists as particles, and particles have energy. They are always moving in some capacity, depending on whether they are a solid, liquid or gas, and on how much energy they have. For example, if you add heat energy to an ice cube, the water particles will gain energy and vibrate faster, breaking some of the forces between one water particle and the next. The result is a change in state from solid to liquid. They are still just water particles, nothing has changed there. However, its structure *has* changed.

You cannot create or destroy energy, which means that the electricity that you are using right now to power your e-reader, or turn on your lights, watch the television, scroll through your phone, or wash your clothes, is not created energy. Electricity became electrical energy first through the chemical energy stored in the fossil fuels being burned at the power station. The chemical energy transfers to heat energy when we burn them. That then causes the kinetic (movement) energy of the water to increase, which causes the water to change state to gas, creating water vapour, or steam. This steam then continues the kinetic energy by turning the turbine. Add some magnets to the mix, and you now transfer the kinetic energy of the moving turbine into electrical energy. We send that through power lines directly into our homes, and you transfer it to light, sound and heat energy, depending on how you are using it.

Why do I drone on about this? Because it is key to understanding the power of the Universe, and this is the energy that is all around us – not created or destroyed, just transferred. It flows around us, through us, and connects us to everything else on this planet, including each other.

This brings me to two major concepts: The power of mindset, and opportunities. Let us look at each fully.

The power of mindset:

If everything on the planet, including us, is vibrating with energy, and energy can have various frequencies, that means we can each be vibrating with a different energy frequency. This is where our mindset comes in. If we are focusing on the negative, always waiting for what seems inevitable and complaining, then that is the frequency at which we will vibrate. That also means we will attract others who are also vibrating at this frequency. Surrounding ourselves with others who are also negative, often complaining, and generally waiting around for bad things to happen, will reinforce these feelings within ourselves. This will cause us to feel like we belong, we are heard, we are validated – like our needs are being met. Of course, this just fuels us and perpetuates our negative energetic flow. You know the expression, 'What you put out there, you will get'? Yes, we have all heard this, because it is so true.

Our negative mindset and belief patterns have a ripple effect on our energy, the people attracted to us and the ones we surround ourselves with, as well as the Universal energy we are attracting. Remember, energy is not created or destroyed. What we put out will return to us. It is like we are screaming to the Universe to tell it this is what we want and need, and it is delivering. Not only is the Universe listening and delivering to us exactly what we have asked for, but when we are faced with positive and attractive opportunities in our lives, we will choose to see them as negative. Why? Because it is unfamiliar and we are creatures of habit. It is uncomfortable to shift our energetic frequency, and we have the tendency to view 'uncomfortable' as 'bad'.

We are going to talk about how to shift this energy into a positive frequency later in this book, but know now that it is very possible.

Opportunities:

We have been talking about the Universal energy that is everywhere; running around us, through us and between us. It connects us to each other, to our Higher Self, and to the Universe. The opportunities provided by the Universe which I mentioned earlier involve this connection. Many people will refer to them at first notice as coincidences. These are the moments when you answer a call to find it is the very person you have been thinking about over the last few days. Or when you just finish having a conversation about something in particular that you need, then find it on sale at your regular supermarket.

We are energetic beings, all of us, and the energy that is all around us also serves to connect us to others. When we are vibrating at a certain frequency, putting our attention into something, that energetic frequency gets passed along, like a hot potato. Suddenly, others whom we are connected with through Universal energy feel the pull of your energetic frequency. Next thing you know, you are having a conversation with your best friend about how you really need a real estate agent you trust, when you bump into your old high school friend who is, you guessed it, a real estate agent!

The Universe is always providing. We speak of it like it is a separate entity, but it is not. It is us. All of us. And it is always working to provide us with exactly what we need.

We are given opportunities every day, many of which we pass up. This is partly because we do not recognise them as opportunities in the moment, and partly because it would be uncomfortable to accept them.

Many times, the opportunity can seem devastating. When I was in my mid-late twenties, I owned a massage therapy clinic, which shared space with a foot clinic. I got along so well with the owner of the other clinic, that she introduced me to my first husband. For a few years it was amazing being able to go to work with someone who became my best friend. I loved my work, its location, and working with good people. We started trying to expand in our little space. We each brought in another practitioner and tried to make it work within our cramped quarters.

I started noticing I was feeling left out. My best friend was enjoying her time with the others so much that they were going out for lunch and forgetting to invite me... or doing that 'pity' invite. Slowly, I began to dislike working there. I owned my clinic and loved my work, but did not like how I felt when at work. My husband and I would speak of it often as I found myself going home in tears many nights of the week. I did not feel like I belonged anymore and did not understand why.

He introduced the idea of me moving my clinic to another location, but I immediately rejected the notion. I was convinced this was just a snag – that we would all find our groove again. Really, I was desperate to stay where I was because the fear of the unknown of moving, and the uncomfortable feelings that brought up were too much.

Fast-forward several months, I felt like I did not belong in my own office, that I had done something wrong to lose someone who was close to me, and that I was not good enough.

And then it happened. The Universe played its hand. You see, I did not realise the shift in the relationships and dynamic at work were my opportunity to look elsewhere. I did not realise my husband suggesting I should leave was another opportunity to investigate this idea. I pushed aside these opportunities for several months until I got the biggest push of them all, a fire.

The office I was fighting so hard to stay at went up in flames. Even as I tip-toed through the rubble and charred remains of my office, my mind was racing with how we could continue. I still wasn't getting it. So, the Universe pushed again.

If I thought there was tension between us before this fire, I was sorely mistaken. The level of bile spewed my way after this fire by the women I had chosen to work alongside was devastating. Any chance of a relationship was clearly gone.

While bawling my eyes out on my husband's shoulder I finally, reluctantly, decided to look for office space elsewhere. The moment I made that decision, relief washed over me. I was free. I was happy. I was strong. And I was still going to work with women who were doing their best to belittle me and wear me down. But now I understood.

This was the push the Universe had to give me to take the opportunity lying right at my feet. I did find another space – one that allowed me to expand to have a Wellness Centre with six treatment rooms, overlooking a lake. In time, and with concerted effort on both sides, my friend and I even mended our relationship.

My point here is that I had the opportunity presented to me in the form of unhappiness. It is very likely the opportunity for me to branch out was there long before I began to feel a divide between us. I was not willing to listen. But the Universe was unwilling to give up on me. The nudges had to turn into shoves, pushes, and finally, into a kick right off the edge of the cliff. I shudder to think what would have come next if I still had not listened.

The question is never whether the opportunities are there. Nope. The question is whether you are willing to recognise them and take them.

• Chapter 4 •

Belief in Self

Belief in the Universe goes hand in hand with belief in your Higher Self. You cannot have one without the other. Let me explain why. Your Higher Self is the consciousness of your spirit. The same spirit who has lived many lives, reincarnating over and over. Essentially, we are still talking about energy. Energy cannot be created or destroyed, just transferred. We understand that when we die, the energy stored in the chemical bonds within us will be transferred back into the soil, perhaps in a few million years, to create fossil fuels. If we are to be cremated, that energy stored in the chemical bonds will be transferred to heat energy.

There is still so much we do not understand about the brain itself, never mind the subconscious mind. Is it possible that it too is made of particles vibrating with a certain frequency of energy? Of course. Everything is made of particles. Does that energy also get transferred in the same ways as the energy within our body? Many people believe it does not. Rather, it continues on as our soul or spirit. That soul then reincarnates later to live another life.

This energy is what I am referring to when I speak of a Higher Self. It is the energy that has and will always be you. And, since it is part of this Universal energy, it is also connected to all things. It is the voice inside your head that tells you to do something, even though you do not understand why. Because it has a plan. Your plan.

When I was in my mid-thirties, after my divorce, I had a sudden urge to go to university and earn a degree. I was still a thriving massage therapist, and loved my work. I did not understand why I had this urge, but I listened because I had learned a lot about taking opportunities when they presented themselves from that fire. Within a couple months of being a full-time university student, while still practising massage therapy, I needed a more specific endgame. I decided if I could not help people through massage therapy any more, I still wanted to help society in some way. Becoming a secondary school teacher became my goal.

I forged on for four years, earning an honours degree in Geography and Environmental Studies, and a Bachelor of Education, all while assuming I would continue to live my life as I was, teaching on the side. But when I was just a month from graduating, a change in the system meant I would have to potentially wait up to four years to get a full-time teaching position in my area.

I thought I would supply teach while maintaining my massage therapy practice, so why this bothered me, I could not understand. But it did. Enough to begin to search for work globally. Within three months, I had packed up my life and was moving abroad to be a full-time science teacher in England.

Except, I hated it. Absolutely, truly and fully. I arrived in England with open arms, ready and excited for my new adventure, and by the fourth month I never wanted to teach again.

Because I was incredibly unhappy, and had learned from that fire, I started to do some soul searching for what I should do. No matter what I did, moving back home just did not feel right. I could not understand it.

It was not until three years later, when I met my now husband and stepsons, that it made sense. I would not have been able to move abroad to England as a massage therapist. I needed to become a teacher to get to England on a work visa. And moving back home was not an option that tickled my fancy, because I needed to be in England to meet my husband and stepsons.

So why was I so unhappy teaching then, if I was in the right place and needed to do this work to get there? Because teaching is not my calling, it is just what I needed to do to get *here*.

Just over two years ago, at the time of writing this book, my husband and I sat down to brainstorm what career move I could make so I could have it all – him, the stepkids, and a career I was proud of. For some reason, I was not drawn to being a massage therapist in England. Strange, considering it was my passion for more than sixteen years.

I had never even read a single blog before, but I heard myself suggest to him that I could write one, but on what?

We had some fun brainstorming things I could write about – travel, recipes, the educational system in the UK. Out of seemingly nowhere, it came to me. I was going to write a blog about my experiences recovering from child abuse. Heavy.

My point here is that I could not have known why I had that initial urge to earn my university degree. But trusting that some part of me knew exactly why, and trusting myself to follow her and be able to handle whatever was to be on the other side of this, created my very ability to write this book now. My life and lifestyle now comes from that decision to listen to my Higher Self and enrol in university. She made me make some tough choices along the way – closing down my business and moving continents to name a couple of huge ones. But I listened, because she *is* me. This was the plan for myself I could not see. And I know, beyond a shadow of a doubt, that I am exactly where I am supposed to be.

I did not always have a firm grasp of Universal energies and connecting to my Higher Self. Like most people, I meandered through life for the first two decades, saying the word 'coincidence' and blaming others for any predicament that caused me pain – particularly my abuser.

But one day, something amazing happened. It may not seem earth-shattering to most, but to me it was the jolt I needed to put me on my correct path. When I was in my very late teens, I was standing at a bus stop on a sunny day. My attention wandered to my thoughts and I caught myself short. I realised my internal dialogue fixated on complaining about the bright, beautiful sunshine. Instead of basking in it, being grateful for its presence, and enjoying its warmth, I was complaining about it being too bright.

That was my moment. I realised who I really was, and I hated it. From that point forward, I began to be sensitive to my thoughts, especially my negative mantra. This caused me to want something different for myself, something better. I immediately began reading self-help books, learning and understanding more about myself and my role in my own life.

Three years later was another huge pinnacle moment for me. I was introduced to Reiki. Prior to this, I had only heard of Reiki, which is energy work, in a presentation given by a classmate at massage therapy school.

As my course was coming to an end and I was preparing to take my licensing exams, I was looking for a way to immediately set me apart from all my competition – essentially, all my classmates that were about to graduate alongside me. A client I had been treating for months in the school clinic came in for one of our last treatments, and randomly began telling me about a Reiki treatment she had earlier in the week. I saw this woman weekly for months, and learned about many aspects of her life, and never once had she spoken about energy or spirituality, or Reiki. But there she was, on my table talking about this amazing experience during her first Reiki treatment. The more she spoke, the more excited I got at the prospect of incorporating this type of modality into my practice to better treat my clients.

I asked every question I could think of, including the therapist's details, and the second she left I reached out to this Reiki practitioner, who was actually a Reiki master. I wasn't interested in a treatment, only the training. I enrolled for her Reiki level one training weekend right there on the spot. There was no way I could have known how much this one decision would impact my life. I thought I was increasing the services I could offer my clients, making me more marketable. I was actually opening the door to my healing journey. After that one weekend, my eyes were opened to the workings of Universal energy and the interconnectedness of all things. Never again would I simply notice a 'coincidence' and brush it off as such.

Opportunity came knocking so hard for me that I completed my Reiki master training within a year. Yes, I incorporated it into my practice as planned, but I also incorporated it into my entire life. Everything I know, and everything I am about to teach you, has stemmed from the understandings I gained after becoming attuned to Universal energy through those Reiki trainings. Not over the course of a single weekend of training, of course, but rather over the course of my newly awakened life.

We are going to talk about how to connect to your Higher Self and the Universe as we move through this book.

• Chapter 5 •

Choosing Our Lessons in Life

Now we have started talking about reincarnation and our Higher Self, let us talk about something fascinating. One of the main reasons people have difficulty believing in a Higher Power is tragedy, especially when defenceless children are at the centre. We all have lessons to learn here in life, otherwise what would be the point? As spiritual, energetic beings, we are learning and growing through every moment in our existence.

It is my belief we had a plan of what those lessons were going to be for this life *before* we entered the world in this form. We tallied everything we learned from previous lives, and set ourselves a course of action that would allow ourselves to build upon those lessons, and in some cases challenge them, just to ensure we really learned them. In other cases, it is very possible we chose *not* to learn lessons in previous lives, and so they are now carried forward to the present.

Having an idea for what we want to learn is great, but without a game plan we would be left roaming around in this life, randomly trying to learn lessons we specifically do not remember needing to learn. That doesn't sound very practical. We are not on this journey alone. We are not just surrounded by Universal energy, angels, spirit guides, and ancestors who have passed before us, but we are also surrounded by people. People who have already pledged their allegiance to us to help us learn our lessons. That also means we have pledged ourselves to others in the same way.

The bottom line is we have made pacts with the subconscious energy of the soul *before* we reincarnated into this life. I do not believe we mapped it all out. No, I believe the *how* of this plan is left up to us, as reincarnated beings, based on our choices in this life. That means when someone is helping us to learn a life lesson, they have free will over how they will do this.

Of course, none of us remember making this pact on a conscious level, so it is not like we are sitting around trying to come up with funny or disturbing ways of 'helping' people with their lessons. As far as we are consciously aware, we are just going about our own business, interacting with other people each day. It does not occur to most of us that our actions and reactions impact others. That impact can be positive or negative – not just because of how you present your actions or reactions, but because of how they are interpreted by others. That is right. We all have our own back-stories and experiences, which cause us to view and interpret the world differently. So, something you interpret to be kind and loving can easily be interpreted by someone else as hateful and spiteful. It is all about perspective. Usually.

There are instances, of course, where there is no positive way to interpret the actions of others. Knowingly causing harm to others, for example. That would be very difficult to interpret in a positive light.

My point here is this: Just because someone has a negative impact on you, does not mean they did not help you to learn a life lesson. They simply chose to do it in a negative way. That is on them, not you. Your choice now is, what are you going to do with this lesson? Will you learn it or dismiss it because of the way it was presented?

Potential Trigger Warning

As you read in the first chapter, when I was two years old, my mother brought my soon-to-be stepfather home. Over the next ten years, this man physically, psychologically, and sexually abused me. He told me every day I was ugly, stupid, worthless, useless and nobody would ever love me. He called me demoralising names like 'Gonzo' after a character on the muppets who had an enormous nose. This man would beat me, throw me down the stairs, choke me, hold me under hot water, and even cut open the skin on my hands and the backs of my ears. When I brought home a test result of an 'A', I would be punished for not getting an 'A+'. Nothing I did was *ever* good enough. During this ten-year period, I do not recall him ever telling me not to tell anyone. He did not have to. Not because I did not realise all this was wrong, but because I thought everyone knew and I was not worth saving. Why?

Because that was the lesson I was learning as a child – I was worthless. I had no value. I was not good enough. For another ten years after we left, I continued this mantra in my head every day, multiple times a day, 'I am ugly, stupid, worthless, useless and nobody will ever love me'.

One day, I was tired of feeling this way. I started on my path of healing the emotional and psychological damage from my abuse. And on this journey, I began to discover the truth: He had taught me a very valuable lesson and it was *not* the words in that mantra. He attempted to teach me my value and worth, just in an extremely negative way. But it was *because* of his choice in teaching me this lesson that I had to dig very deep and find my true value and worth. I learned my lesson. I learned I am a valuable human worthy and deserving of love, both of myself and from others. Realising we would have made a pact to help me learn this lesson gave me my power back and allowed me to move on and truly heal. His choice to hurt me so badly was all about him, not me. *My* choice was what I was going to do with this experience. What did I want to learn from it? What did I deserve to learn from it?

There is not a person alive who has not been presented with help to learn their life lessons in a negative way. But there are many people who will choose to dismiss their lesson because of the way it was presented to them. The lesson will not disappear. Instead, if we choose not to learn our lesson in this life, it will be carried forward in the next.

This was a tremendous motivator for me. When all this information came to light I thought to myself, 'Holy crap, how will this lesson be presented in the next life if in this one it was *this* horrible?' I had a vision of getting baby nudges in each life, culminating in this life. I could not imagine what my next life was going to entail if I did not learn my lesson in this one.

I was petrified! I was also motivated, because once this world of Universal connection to my Higher Self and others was made clear to me, I fully understood that self-hating and self-deprecation could never be my lesson in life. Crucially, I took the time and self-reflection I needed to discover the true lesson from my experiences.

Take some time to briefly revisit some of the most negative experiences in your life, with the loving support you deserve, and ponder what the positive lesson could have been. Take the negativity away for a moment, and try to see the original endgame. What lesson did you learn from the experience? Do you believe that is the lesson you designed for yourself – which the Universe and your Higher Self have been helping you learn? Or, is it possible there is a much more positive lesson buried deep below and your 'teacher' was just choosing to help you learn this lesson in a negative way?

In the following chapter, we will look at how to use this concept to forgive.

• Chapter 6 •

The Power of Forgiveness

So, we have talked openly about the lessons we are here to learn. More importantly, we talked about the people who are here to help us learn those lessons and how they do not always teach us in a positive way.

Now, let us talk about potentially one of the most difficult things to do – forgive. To forgive does not mean we are saying what happened was acceptable. It also does not mean we will forget. Forgiveness is about acknowledging and accepting what happened. This is a crucial step in finding our strength, not despite what happened, but *because* of it. Our greatest strength can be found deep within our weakness, but only if we find it.

Forgiving my abuser was not about resigning myself to thinking what he did was acceptable. It was about understanding his abuse stemmed from his own issues. Him abusing me was about him, his life, experiences and choices. I was just there. And if I wasn't there, someone else would have been. He was not attacking *me* – he was *attacking*.

Truly understanding that he was ultimately opening the door for me to learn my greatest life lesson, allowed me to see the experience from different eyes. I believe before reincarnating into this life, I agreed to have him placed in my life and to help me learn my priceless lesson of self-worth. And I believe neither of us consciously remembered such an agreement. So, he had a choice – teach me in the positive, or in the negative. He had his own life experiences before he was introduced to me. He brought his own experiences into his relationship with my mother, and with me, such as anger and the need to control. *It wasn't about me!*

That being said, I am never going to seek him out and thank him for teaching me such a valuable lesson. That is not what forgiveness of this magnitude is about. Ultimately, he *did not* teach me the lesson at all. Instead, he provided me with the opportunity to teach it to myself.

His abuse left me so vulnerable and shattered, I could have easily allowed that to be my life. And I did, for another decade and some. But when I decided enough was enough, *I* crawled out of that hole. He was not there offering up a hand to grab. *I* used *my own* mental, emotional, and spiritual strength.

I would not have needed to fight so hard to get out of the hole if I had not been thrown into it in the first place. I found my strength *because* of my greatest weakness. And he was the cause of that weakness.

Now, being a believer in the Universe, reincarnation and our life lessons, I know if he had never come into my life, this would still have been my life lesson. Someone else would have risen to the challenge and attempted to help me learn my value and worth. And they may have gone about it in a totally different way. They may have been loving and supportive, giving me the safe childhood every young being deserves. But they were not placed in my life – he was. I cannot change that, but I can accept it. These were the cards I was dealt, so to speak.

I can now choose to carry this feeling of victimisation around with me for all eternity, or I can forgive him. By forgiving him I am really forgiving his inability to remember his vow to help me with my life lesson, and his choice to teach me this lesson in the negative. I am also forgiving myself for my own inability to see the lesson for so long, and to find strength in my journey to teach myself my life lesson. This allows me to release myself from my previous attachment to him. If I agreed to have this soul be such an integral part of this life, then he must be of some importance to my Higher Self. Rather than hate him for what he has done, forgiving and releasing him honours our agreement, and thus my Higher Self. I do not need to know and understand everything. I just need to trust in myself – my Higher Self, and the Universe.

The next chapter will introduce the concept of control, and shed some light on how the need for control can halt our healing and growth.

• Chapter 7 •

Control vs. Power

Control, and our need for it, is at the root of the majority of our issues and inability to grow and heal. Think about it. Anxiety is a wonderful example of the devastation that can be caused by a feeling of lack of control. At the heart of our need for control is fear – fear of the unknown, fear of failure, fear of being hurt, fear of success.

If you suffer with anxiety, or live with someone who does, you know things are not always what they appear. You may find them scrubbing the floors in the middle of the night, or demanding things be done around the home in a very specific way. They may seem to 'go off' without notice, leaving everyone to walk on eggshells. This is what a lack of control looks like. They are acting in this way because they are reacting to their feeling of being powerless. Taking control in any way they can is making them feel like they have regained their power. When we feel in control, we feel strong and powerful, so we believe the two are interchangeable. When we feel we have a lack of control, we get anxious and fearful and begin to do what we must to gain control wherever we can.

During my ten years of child abuse, I had no control. First, I was only a child, aged between two and twelve. Second, my abuser was overpowering me on a daily basis. I had no control over the words he spoke to me, the beatings, or whether or not he entered my room at night. However, I did learn how to gain control in very small ways. My control came from my ability to 'sense' the tension in the room, reading the situation. I became very attuned with his energy. I could walk into a room, sense his mood, and adjust to ease the situation to prevent beatings or verbal lashings.

Of course, this did not work all of the time, but when it did, *I* felt I had control. In learning how to do this, potentially saving me from countless other beatings, I brought this skill into my adulthood. The coping strategy was effective at getting me what I wanted and needed, safety, so I implemented it long after I was removed from that unsafe environment. As we learned at the beginning of this book, I was getting my needs met as best I could.

Here is the problem with continuing this strategy long after the need for it has passed – it assumes I still have no control, which renders me powerless. By attempting to grasp small chunks of the control pie when I could, I was putting myself (and my energy) in a place of lacking control in the first place. That feeling of lack of control was now driving my every action and reaction, attempting to gain back control and, ultimately, my power. I constantly surrounded myself with people I believed had the control I craved because it was intoxicating.

'If I cannot have control, or power, then I will surround myself with those that do.'

I would seek out male companions who were not emotionally able to commit to me, because I thought if someone like that could love me, then I must be loveable. That was my way of gaining control when I did not believe I deserved it in the first place. This train of thought complements the vicious cycle I was in – my internal battle between wanting control and not believing I had or deserved any.

Of course, being so young surrounded by other young people who desperately longed to stay in control at all costs, meant I was constantly living in the negative. I could not grow or heal because I lacked understanding of the difference, and interconnectedness, of control and power. 'Power' does not come from *overpowering* or *controlling* others. True power lies in this understanding: You cannot control the actions or reactions of others. You can only control your own actions and reactions in every situation. I did not have control over what was happening in my home during my childhood. But I do have control over my actions and reactions to it now. I can choose to let it continue to devastate me, or I can choose to rise above it and learn my lessons from it. That choice is my power.

We can apply this to absolutely any situation in our lives. You cannot control the words your employer chooses to use on a daily basis, but you can be aware of how his/her words are affecting you. You can then make a *choice* on how you are willing to allow those words to affect you, and regain your power. Eliminating control allows you to gain power.

These are the choices we are faced with in every moment of every day. And while this may make perfect sense and excite you with a new desire to try this out, you will still attempt to vie for control. It is human nature, really. It is what makes us feel prepared for anything, which makes us feel less anxious.

Here is a relatively simple exercise you can do daily to relinquish control: Surrender your need to control, and your fear of a lack of control, to the Universe. This can be done during meditation, or can be a prayer, positive intention/affirmation, or conversation you have with the Universe. Imagine yourself taking your fears and need for control and boxing them up. Place that box into a basket and offer it up to the Universe, using a mantra you feel drawn to. For example, while offering up the basket you can say, 'I surrender my need for control, and the fear that comes with it, to the Universe. I trust that the Universe is always working for my Highest good. I have no need for this control or fear as I am one with the Universe, surrounded by Divine wisdom and love'. You can even visualise an angel floating down to retrieve the basket, and watch them fly off out of sight with it, knowing your fears and need for control are released.

Surrendering your fears and need for control is not the only thing you can hand over to the Universe. In fact, you will find fear and control at the centre of nearly all your issues, but they can take the form of other things. Whenever you find yourself so invested in an outcome, worrying, or problem-solving for situations that have not even occurred yet, release it all to the Universe.

Creating new habits can seem almost impossible. That is because we often get distracted and do not stick with it long enough to make it an actual new habit. Surrendering your need to control, and your fears, to the Universe is a new habit. It will take time to instil. In fact, depending on the source, a new habit can take between twenty-one and sixty-six days to set.

I recommend you begin this challenge by combining this release with daily meditation, or a self-reflection activity. Set aside a small amount of time every day.

Now, before you tell me you do not have time for that, may I gently remind you that we **always** *find* the time for things that are important to us. You are important. 'Nough said!

• Chapter 8 •

Failure or Redirection?

Whenever something does not go the way we planned, we instantly feel we have failed. We build up this image of what our success will look like in our minds, many times with intricate detail. Perhaps it is our reaction to something, or someone's reaction to us. Maybe it is something very important to us, like a relationship breaking down that we expected to always be loving, safe and secure. Or a job promotion that went to someone else after we laboured to get it. It could be something as enormous as our very life itself. We had grand plans for what we would be, when we would marry, how many children we would have, and how happy our life would be. We planned out every single detail, or at least had hopes and expectations for how things would unfold. And then... they do not.

Whatever 'it' is, it just does not happen the way we wanted it to. This happens every single day, great or small, to all of us.

For some, things not working out to plan can seem like constant disappointment. It can leave you feeling that, when something good happens, something bad will follow.

These feelings can begin to slowly create an expectation of failure, and even a fear of success. It is also the basis for many people's lack of belief in a Higher

Power. You know you are a good person, and you know your heart is in the right place, yet you never seem to get a break. It wears you down. You begin to develop feelings of unworthiness, like you do not deserve to be happy. Sometimes, you may even begin to believe you are being punished.

When you truly connect with the Universe and your Higher Self, you start to realise at your core that can never be the truth. What if, instead of leading a disappointing life where things never turn out the way you planned, leaving you feeling like a failure and like you are not good enough, you began to look at things differently? What if each disappointment or failure was really an *opportunity* for redirection? Is it possible that your plan, while it was made with good intentions and made you feel good to think about its outcome, would not serve your Highest good? Perhaps things not going according to that plan was the opportunity the Universe and your Higher Self were placing before you to take notice and shift, to meet your needs while serving your Highest good?

It is natural for us to reject the change, or the shift. After all, you worked so hard to plan and reach this goal. Changing strategies, tactics, or the goal itself midway through seems ridiculous. But here is what we must understand: We have the power to see what we want to see and interpret things as best suits us in that moment. If we want and need to see failure, that will be our interpretation, no matter what.

Have you ever had something go exactly according to plan yet you still couldn't rejoice in the success because you were so busy reflecting upon some little details you wished would have been different? You are not letting yourself succeed even when you have clearly been successful. You are intent on finding failure in that moment.

The very hard lesson here is: That this is *your choice.* You have a plan for yourself in this life: goals you are here to reach, lessons you are here to learn, and lessons you are here to help others learn. When something seems to not be working out the way you wanted it to, take comfort in the knowledge the Universe and your Higher Self are working hard to help guide you towards reaching your goals and learning and teaching your lessons. While your plan was made with love in your heart, your conscious mind has long forgotten your goals, lessons, and pacts you have made with other souls. Whenever we begin veering off our path, the Universe and our Higher Self will always be there to steer us back. Looking at it in this way, failure is impossible. If you are willing to stay in the present, notice any opportunities, and grab hold of them, you will never fail at anything. You will have been redirected.

When I was in my early twenties, I had the opportunity to take over the massage therapy clinic I spoke about at the beginning of this book. It came as I accepted a job offer to work with Club Med. I had a choice to make, and knew I had to follow my intuition, which told me to stay and build my practice.

Starting small by taking over the one treatment room in the shared office, I built my business from the ground up. Eventually, I was ready to expand and I moved my office, changed its name and reopened as a large Wellness Centre with multiple types of therapies. (This move in itself was due to a huge push, or opportunity, presented to me by the Universe which I discussed earlier in the book). Five years later, with a thriving practice, I was unhappy. I had been practising massage therapy for ten years, five of them being in this beautiful space along the lake, and I was no longer filled with joy.

I even had lots of money. Still, I felt like I was failing at work because, by owning the Wellness Centre, all my attention was going into the practicalities of running a business instead of into my clients.

I had a strong desire to begin working from home, but that would mean closing down my Wellness Centre. Worry began to set in. It was not just me at the Wellness Centre. I had many other practitioners working there. Where would they go? Would they be okay? What if I did not like working from home? Heck, my home was not even designed to be suitable – having clients coming into my personal space yet allowing them to feel welcome and comfortable. Also, closing the centre would feel like I had failed.

Still, I could not shake the feeling I needed this change. I had a choice now to listen or ignore. I chose to listen, closed down my centre confident that all the practitioners would find their way to where they were supposed to be next, and opened my home-based business.

It was not ideal. Clients had to walk through my front door, through my entire home to my spare room in the back, then make their payment and next booking standing in my kitchen! I saw the look on some of their faces. In some, I heard the undertone in their questions on why I had to shut down my Wellness Centre. *They* thought I had failed. Still, I was choosing to see it as an opportunity instead of a failure. The problem was, I did not know exactly what the opportunity was.

Here is where it gets interesting. Less than one month into me working from home, my husband and I separated. This was a shock. We both thought we were unbreakable. We learned the hard way that was not true. We had fertility problems, and like many couples suffering with infertility, it took a toll on our marriage. For our five years of fertility battles, I felt like I was a failure – that I would be such a terrible mother that no soul wanted to reincarnate into being *my* child.

Eventually, I started to accept my life as being motherless, redirecting my energies towards helping society in other ways. I had a notion working from home would somehow allow this, I just could not figure out how.

Within nine months of our separation, I needed to buy and renovate another home so I could move myself and my business. I never would have been able to afford that if I was still carrying the cost of the very large

Wellness Centre. And the feeling of failure due to the loss of my marriage? Eventually, I ended up moving to another continent. Six years after my divorce, while living abroad, I met my now husband and his two sons.

I am blessed with children in my life, and I know I am in their lives to help them learn their life lessons, as much as they are in my life to help me with mine. Having children with my first husband would not have served my Highest good. I was not ready then. I was not in the right place, or with the right person. Now, I am helping society to the fullest of my abilities by the work I do, and I get to be a stepmother to two amazing boys. I am exactly where I need to be, and I am here *because* of all the redirections in my life.

At each stage of my story, I had no idea why things were happening, and not always did I have faith they were happening for a reason, to serve my Highest good. But I made the best decisions I could at each stage, looked for the possible opportunities, and when I recognised them, I took them. Eventually, it all came together and made perfect sense. Everything that has ever happened to you, or ever will happen to you, is an opportunity. You have the power to trust in this and take the opportunities as they come, knowing they will lead you to where you need to be, even though you do not yet understand how or even why. Or, you can dismiss them, allowing yourself to feel like you are failing, being punished, and are not worthy of being happy.

When in doubt, surrender your fear of the unknown to the Universe, saying, 'I surrender my fear to the Universe. I trust that the Universe is always working for my Highest good. I have no need for fear as I am one with the Universe, surrounded by Divine wisdom and love.'

I would also recommend you begin logging your opportunities. Start with writing down difficult situations you have been in, followed by how you can now see how those experiences guided you to where you are now.

When you are comfortable with that exercise, extend it to current opportunities. Take some time at the end of each day to reflect on it. Write down all the scenarios from your day. For example, you might write how you felt when your boss called upon you at a meeting, how you ran into an old friend at the supermarket, and how you got frustrated while making dinner for your family.

In many cases, every day, you will not know what the opportunity is. You have to trust that there *is* one, which will eventually reveal its purpose. That being said, for each of your scenarios, write in the possible opportunity. This doesn't have to be correct. It is more of an exercise to get you to change your perspective, looking out for opportunities each day. For example, you may determine that you felt nervous when your boss called upon you during the meeting because he always makes you feel like you are not good enough. Are these feelings of low worth something you can work on? Perhaps the old friend you ran into at the supermarket is a counsellor now and can point you in the right direction for one-on-one support with your self-esteem? And finally, getting frustrated while making dinner for your family may be a call for you to take the time to voice your need for help with your family. Perhaps it is an opportunity to beef up the chores list for the kids, and have a heartfelt conversation with your husband about helping each other, so all needs are being met.

I will give you a great example. A client was dealing with some deep-rooted anger issues. She was a ball of fury. The problem was, even though it was so obvious to me and others around her, she could not see it.

She went to the supermarket after work one day and ran into an old high school friend she had not seen for fifteen years. They had once been great friends, so she was so excited to have run into her. While they did not have time then to go for coffee, they exchanged business cards so they could plan for another time. When my client got to her car and looked at her friend's business card, she discovered her friend is now an anger management counsellor.

When my client got home with the weekly food shop, she opened the door to her beautiful home to find her children and husband in an enormous battle. They had been fighting for quite some time. The children had been physically fighting with one another, and she walked in when her husband was at his breaking point. In his efforts to break up the fight, he was red-faced, veins throbbing, and screaming at the top of his lungs.

She was taken aback, not just because this was so unusual – her children normally get along quite well and her husband has the patience of an angel – but because this was the first time she felt a mirror had been held up to her face. This was her. Her children fighting was her daily, internal struggle. Her husband's red face and screaming voice was how she felt deep inside, every day.

She knew in that moment she had run into her friend so she would have the support she needed when she realised her own deep-rooted anger. And that is exactly what she did. She dropped everything and called her friend, asking for a referral for anger management.

Living a life you deserve is not about life being perfect. It is about having true faith in yourself, your Higher Self, and the Universe to know for certain you will always be taken care of. It is knowing that when you begin to veer, the Universe will be there to steer. You just have to believe you deserve it. When you do, you will understand at your core being, there is no such thing as failure. There are always opportunities for redirection on to your correct path.

• Chapter 9 •

Becoming Your Own Hero

A great way to begin your journey towards changing your life is to begin shifting your mindset. This does not simply refer to learning to have a positive attitude, because having a positive attitude in itself is not enough. Shifting your mindset begins with acknowledging, accepting, and embracing the huge role you are playing in your life.

Truth be told, we have already begun this work throughout this book, with each and every chapter. We have looked at the role of Universal energy and our belief and acceptance of it, and the role of forgiveness, understanding our life lessons, and our choices, and how to shift the notion of failure into redirection. Because each chapter has required you to begin looking at things differently, you are already on your way to shifting your mindset. You have started your journey towards understanding the role your thoughts, actions and reactions play in your life. You have started to take responsibility. This means this is the perfect spot for this chapter.

So many of us have negative thoughts and feelings about ourselves. Naturally, we look to find acceptance within others. If people enjoy our company, want to date or marry us, have children with us, shower us with compliments and treat us like we are the most amazing person on the planet, we will start to believe it. That is exactly why we will *never* believe it.

There is an expression, 'Seeing is believing'. However, while having evidence of something is important, this expression implies that in order to believe it, you have to see it first. Rather, I am convinced if you do not believe something, you will not *allow* yourself to see it. My expression, then, is, 'Believing is seeing'.

Take our example from above. If you are relying on someone else to show you your worth and value, not believing it to be so unless and until they show you, do you really think you will believe them when they do? First of all, if you do not believe in your own value and worth, you are probably attracting others more than willing to show you that you have none. But even when you do have someone wanting to show you how special you are, you are more likely to wonder what he has done wrong and be uncomfortable with his affections than you are to accept them.

When I was in my early twenties, I was going through boyfriends quite quickly. I thought I was standing up for myself, kicking all those who did not deserve me to the kerb. A dear friend of mine pulled me aside one day to ask me what I was doing. In her opinion, I had a few great contenders for a serious relationship I had thrown away, and she could not understand it. She had seen one young man in particular bring me flowers for no occasion, call me daily, want to spend time with me, and treat me with adoring affection. I thought my explanation as to why he had to go would make sense as I proudly informed her of all the things I had wanted him to say and do that he had not.

I was shocked at her response. She gasped in horror.

'Oh yes, he is not the angel you thought he was!' I exclaimed.

My smugness was wiped off my face when she pointed out that just because he had not used the exact words I wanted him to, or done some things the exact way I wanted them done, did not mean he did not love and respect me.

Her exact words were, 'He is not psychic!'

That incident slowly made me realise I was setting myself up for failure by expecting very specific words and actions from someone to 'prove' their affections. It is not that I did not deserve to be treated with love. More that I would not allow myself to see my worth within others because I did not believe in it myself. How could someone say the exact things I wanted him to say to prove my value? The bottom line was, I was looking for a knight in shining armour to save me, while at the same time making it impossible for him to find me. I was never going to find my value within someone else. My value and worth needed to be found by me, within me. Once I truly believed in my value and worth, then, and only then, could I see it being expressed in others. I could accept someone telling me how much they love me and enjoy my company, using whatever words or actions they wanted to use.

To truly shift your mindset, you too need to take responsibility for your actions. You need to learn to become your own knight in shining armour. Becoming your own hero is about believing *and then* seeing.

So how do you do this? In our next chapter we will talk extensively about how our daily choices are influenced by our belief systems, finding the evidence to prove them right or wrong, and how to rewrite the script.

• Chapter 10 •

Rewrite the Script

We make countless decisions every day. The thought of it is exhausting. Most of our decisions are made by our subconscious, or they are decisions we do not give a lot of conscious thought to.

Many of the decisions, we make out of fear. Fear of failure. Fear of not being good enough. Fear of being called out. Fear of success.

Many more are made in haste – you are standing in the line at the checkout, in a rush, no make-up on, wearing your sweats because you were just running out to grab something quick, when you spot someone you know. Ugh. Your first reaction is usually to look away and pretend you did not see them, praying they did not see you. It is not just because you are too busy to talk. You are standing in a line. You have time. You fear their judgement.

Perhaps you fear they may judge your level of success by your looks, choice of outfit, frazzled emotional state assumed by your lack of make-up, and your answers to very important questions about your life.

Why? First, why do you care what they think? Will their perception of you spill out on to the floor, climb up your legs, and latch on to you until it becomes truth? Second, why would they be judging? Is everyone else all put together, having a perfect life, while you are a complete mess?

You are fearing their judgement because you are judging yourself. All these fears are a projection of how you truly see yourself. That fear, and the belief system that started it, will be the reason you successfully look away, do not attract attention to yourself, and miss the opportunity standing right in front of you to talk to that person.

The way you look at your life, your accomplishments, your misses, your near-misses, all of it, is a choice. You are making a choice to see things through the eyes of your deepest belief systems.

The natural question then is, what do you believe? Taking a very hard look at what you believe about yourself – your value, worth, ability, strength – as well as your beliefs about family, success, failure, and money are all impacting every single decision you make, every day.

For example, growing up as a middle-class white girl in a city known for its steel production, I always heard the adults in my life referring to people with money as 'filthy, stinking rich'. There were always digs aimed at the values, work ethic, and humanity of wealthy people. In short, the adults in my life thought to have money meant you must lie, cheat and steal to get it. It was also ingrained in me you had to work extremely hard to earn money, and regardless of how much you earned, you never had enough.

These ideas about money became my deeply-rooted belief system. As I grew up and got a job, my subconscious always found a way to get rid of any money I earned. I was living pay cheque to pay cheque, not because I was not working hard or did not know how to balance a cheque book, but because at the core, I did not believe having money was a good thing. My belief money was filthy, and to have it meant I was a crook, fuelled my decisions to spend, spend, spend. Get rid of the filth!

To change this pattern, I had to get real. I needed to discover, then confront, this belief system. The first thing I did was to find some positive role models surrounding money. I began not only looking at celebrities using their money to make a difference on a global scale with humanitarian efforts, but at 'real' people in my life.

It turns out, there were several people in my life who had much more money than me, and seemed to respect it enough to keep it around. Some of these people were also the most generous, kind, and caring people I have ever known. Just allowing myself to realise that dispelled several money myths. They showed me you can earn money honestly and be a wonderful human being. Perhaps they could not contribute as much as the wealthiest celebrities, but they were contributing towards major causes near and dear to them.

That was not all I had to do to change my relationship with money. I had other belief systems that were getting in the way of me earning and keeping money. Belief systems about my worth, and what I deserved.

For a long time after I was safe from my abuser, I played his mantra daily. I believed those words. After all, he had spoken them to me nearly every day for ten years. Believing I was ugly, stupid, worthless, useless, nobody would ever love me and I would never amount to anything equated to me truly believing I deserved that treatment. I believed I deserved it from others and I believed I deserved it from myself. That meant each time I was using money as a measure of success, I immediately made decisions that would cause me to lose that money. After all, at the core, I believed I did not deserve that success, or by extension, that money.

Just as I had done with finding positive money role models and dispelling the money myths, I needed to now dispel the negative beliefs about myself. To do this, I looked at each belief separately, and countered it with real-life examples proving that belief wrong. For example, my belief I was stupid was dispelled when I allowed myself to acknowledge how well I had always done in school. The belief I had no value could be dispelled by my friendship circle – the fact I had one was proof I meant something to someone. I also allowed myself to feel pride about the work I had done to help others. This allowed me to realise I had positively impacted other people, so my life had value.

After doing this exercise for each of my belief systems, I was able to realise the subconscious influence they had been having over every decision I made. I realised I had a choice: continue on with business as usual, or fight for a new belief. And that is my point. I made the choice to rewrite my script, but I could just as easily have made the choice to stay in my downward spiral of self-sabotage. There is *always* a choice. Most times, the choice that will serve your Highest good is the one that requires the most effort. If you make the choice to put in the effort, you will see great rewards. You cannot expect to see a change in results if your methods remain the same.

We will use the remainder of this book to tackle those methods. Let us dive in and see how you can make some life-altering changes to your day, and to your life.

• Chapter 11 •

Positive Intentions and Affirmations

What is the difference between setting an intention versus an affirmation? Wikipedia gives a great definition and explanation of each that I endorse. It states that setting an intention is representative of the commitment to carrying out an action, including planning and thinking ahead. An example is, 'I intend to be positive today'. Whereas an affirmation is a declaration something is true. They are usually seen as 'I am' statements. For example, 'I am naturally positive'. We will blur the lines here, while talking about each.

If I asked you to write down everything you could do for yourself, your growth, and your healing every day, without having to worry about time management and other responsibilities, I bet your list would be large. What I hear often from my students and clients is how they 'would' do this or that. It is very rare to hear someone come from a place of action and proudly exclaim they 'will' do this or that. Until they are prompted, of course.

There is a big difference. Saying you 'would' do something is allowing you to plan to fail. You can see it, can you not? 'I *would* do that, BUT...'

When you come from a place of action, by saying 'I will do this', you are driven, like you have every intention of doing it.

So why do you not use active language more? There are too many reasons to list here, but they all come down to one thing... You do not believe you are worth it. You are so wrapped up in the logistics of it, of making all the excuses, to hide from the truth – you do not believe you are worth it.

I get it. In an ideal world you would meditate daily for thirty to sixty minutes, spend time on your physical, emotional and spiritual health, and would build the life of your dreams. You are not doing these things not because of the excuses you have been telling yourself. You know, the ones that go a little something like: 'I do not have time to meditate daily, never mind for thirty to sixty minutes!' 'I do not have the time or resources to work on my physical, emotional and spiritual fitness.' 'I have been working hard all my life, and I never get close to my dream life.'

Deep down, you do not believe you are worth physical, emotional and spiritual stability, that you are worth that dream life you have been longing for.

Let me ask you this: If your car broke down, would you do what you had to, to get it repaired? Would you bring it to the shop for proper repairs, use the money from your savings, or save the money for the repair? I am betting you are like me and you have given a resounding 'Yes, duh! Of course, I *need* my car.' Well, if your car deserves to be healthy, surely you do. I am here to tell you that you are worth the time; you do have control over your actions and reactions; you do have the power to make better decisions; and you can have everything you feel you deserve. YOU are the solution to this problem.

We have spoken throughout this book about energy. So far, I have outlined that all things are made of particles and all particles vibrate with energy. Different amounts of energy will lead to different energy vibration frequencies. We talked about how you attract others vibrating with the same frequency, which gives you a sense of acceptance. And we also talked about energy not being created or destroyed but, rather, transferred. This is all very important and is an underlying theme throughout this book for a reason. When we attempt to shift our energy, by changing our habits and thought patterns, it pulls us out of our comfort zone and feels 'wrong'.

Try this experiment for me. Quickly, without thinking about it, clasp your hands together, interlacing your fingers, in your lap. This is normal, right? Anybody walking by would notice you have your hands clasped in your lap and would not think twice about it. This is the analogy of your comfort zone and your energy vibration within it.

Now, unclasp your hands, holding them in a straight prayer position, and slide just one hand slightly forward so your fingers are no longer lined up. Without shifting them back, clasp your hands again from this new position. It feels terrible, does it not? There is absolutely nothing wrong with it. The only difference is your fingers are placed one finger position ahead. That is it. Someone walking by would notice your hands clasped in your lap and think nothing of it. Yet every fibre of your being is screaming at you to 'put them back!'

This is the perfect analogy for your target comfort zone and your energy vibration as you attempt to reach it. Vibrating at a different frequency from your 'normal' is palpable. And it does not feel great. At first. If you repeat this activity at the start of every day for the next week, you will see how comfortable you will eventually get with this new hand-clasp position.

That is the point. It takes determined effort, over time. As I have mentioned before, new habits take anywhere from twenty-one to sixty-six days to instil, most experts agree. Shifting your mindset and changing your beliefs takes effort and time. This whole analogy is the third most important reason why it is so easy to fall back into your old patterns – it takes time for the new energy vibration to feel 'normal'. The second most important reason is because you do not have a plan. And the number one reason is the belief you do not deserve it.

So, let us change all of it. In one sweep, let us systematically deal with each of these issues so you can finally make the changes you want and deserve. Setting positive intentions and affirmations is a fantastic and easy way to shift your vibration from negative to positive. Of course, there are loads of intentions and affirmations you can find through the internet, but ultimately you want to find some that resonate with you and your situation. This may require you to create your own, or at least tweak those you find on the internet.

When creating your own affirmation, you can begin by writing out the polar opposite of a negative thought or belief you have about yourself or a situation. For example, if you have a negative mantra running through your mind that you are stupid, your affirmation can be 'I am a highly intelligent and capable person'. It is literally the opposite of the original thought.

You can always build on it from there, getting more specific as you get more confident and comfortable. Now, this may seem redundant, but your positive intentions and affirmations need to be positive. Rather than focusing on what you do not want, change the language to focus on what you *do* want. Rather than saying, 'I will not overreact in bad situations today', you could say, 'I will act and react in ways that will serve my Highest good'. Do you see the difference?

If you have something very specific you are working on, you can make your intention or affirmation very specific to match. However, if you do not know the specifics and want to keep it very general and open-ended, you are free to do that also.

It is also important to note here that one positive intention or affirmation could apply to multiple situations. What really matters is how you feel when you say or think about it. For example, 'I see the beauty in all things' can be used during times of frustration, anger, sadness, fear or being overwhelmed. You could use it during conversations, meetings, at work, home, driving. And you can also use it in times of calm, to remind you to take the time to be grateful and fully appreciate the moment.

Ideally, positive intentions should be set in the morning to allow yourself to start the day vibrating at a positive frequency. Affirmations can be used in more spur-of-the-moment situations throughout the day (see below).

If this is new to you, I would recommend you search for some intentions to use from the internet, and start slow. Set one intention each morning as you are getting ready for your day. Once you are comfortable with this, add in ten minutes of time for meditation each morning where you can repeat or think about your intention.

Now, before you start telling me why you do not have time in the mornings, or any time in your day, I am going to remind you that you make time for all other things and people who are important. If your car broke down, not only would you find the funds for its repair, but you would find the time to get it to the garage for the repair. If your child hurt themselves, you would find the time to take them to the hospital, and all the rehab appointments they would need, for as long as they needed them. Find the time. You are worth it.

Now that excuse is dealt with. Once you have been meditating with your intention, start adding more intentions. Simultaneously, you can begin revisiting your intention throughout the day, especially when faced with situations or emotions suited to your intention – the change you want to make.

Eventually, when you are comfortable, you can begin to use new intentions and affirmations as the day unfolds, moment to moment. This is usually where I pull in my go-to intentions or affirmations that seem to cover any situation. I often use affirmations to reaffirm my intentions, or when I am in a spur-of-the-moment situation.

For example, if I am talking to someone and feel a lack of confidence, it is easier to say to myself, 'I am confident', rather than 'My intention is to be confident'.

If I am dealing with a confidence issue on a regular basis, then I will set the intention, 'My intention is to be confident', each morning through meditation, reminding myself of it several times throughout the day.

In this way, positive intentions and affirmations are one and the same – just with a small word shift.

Here are some of my favourites that I have worded as affirmations, but can easily be turned into intentions by adding the prefix 'My intention is to…':

I will find humour in my day, and appreciate each of those moments.

I will remain positive today, allowing myself to flourish with positive thoughts and experiences.

I surround myself with positive, supportive and loving people who mirror my own intentions.

I feel safe and secure in my life. I will approach new experiences today secure in this knowledge.

I am a strong, vibrant person who deserves the best life has to offer.

I am worthy of success and abundance.

• Chapter 12 •

Yoga: Connecting Mind and Body

One of the many ways I coped with my ten years of child abuse was through detaching my mind from my body.

At times it did feel quite literal. It felt like an out-of-body experience, where I was on the other side of the room watching what was happening to my body. I suppose it was my way of protecting my young mind. It definitely felt as though my body was separate from my mind, and whatever happened to it did not matter as much, as long as 'I' was protected.

This was an excellent way for me to cope. To this day, I can speak openly about much of my abuse as if it was someone else's story. I walk away unscathed from the memories, because it is like they are not even mine. The problem with this coping mechanism is having the ability to draw the line. Which I did not. The line between detaching to cope with the atrocities I was facing at home, and dealing with my everyday life – friendships, school work, family relationships, boyfriends, hobbies, you name it – was too fine for me to recognise. So I detached from everything. Right down to myself and my own life. My body was going through the motions, while my soul was elsewhere, protected. Protected from what? Life.

I had been a dancer growing up – mainly jazz, but also tap, ballet and contemporary. I had many injuries, all of which I pushed through, continuing to dance despite the obvious difficulty the injuries could cause. It was not because I was so determined to be on that stage and perform – despite that being my truth. It was not even because I loved dancing, which came as easy to me as breathing – also completely true. It was because my body, which had suffered the injury, was separate from my mind, which was on the stage performing. Any pain I had ever felt in my body had been very, very bad. The beatings I endured during my abuse, along with the seemingly comforting hand on my shoulder, which really signalled I was going to pay a price once we were alone, all taught me that pain equals needing to fight for my survival. I wasn't allowing myself to feel the pain of my dance injuries because I was not allowing myself to feel *anything*. To feel something, especially pain, meant I could die. That is how that computed in my brain, because of my past experience.

I was not just ignoring the feeling of pain though. I was ignoring all feeling, including emotions, for all the same reasons – they hurt, and pain meant life or death. It meant I could walk away from relationships and friendships without batting an eye.

There was a time when I thought this was an excellent skill – the ability to not get attached to people, cutting them off like they were nothing. Until I realised I was not allowing myself the beauty of true relationships because I was never really committing myself.

When I first began my healing journey towards changing my life to become a true survivor, and even a warrior, I kept reaching massive roadblocks. I eventually came to realise I was not going to fully heal until I allowed myself to *feel* again. That was terrifying.

Without consciously thinking about it, I ended up in a yoga studio. At first, I was there to keep in shape and stay limber since I was no longer dancing. I was also there to win. I would roll out my mat, taking a look around the room at my competition, and talk myself up in my head. I would tell myself how impressed everyone would be when they saw my flexibility and strength. As the practice would unfold, I would spend my time peeking around the room to compare myself with others. If someone else was doing well, I would up my game to match their ability. After all, that is what you do as a dancer – the group needs to dance as one. You train to match your ability to the others in your performance group. Basically, I was there for all the wrong reasons and I was doing my best definitely for the wrong reasons.

Eventually, slowly, I began to learn. The instructor would demonstrate a difficult pose that was new to me, and I would struggle. She would come over to assist me and push me further into the pose, causing me discomfort, not pain. My immediate reaction was to block those feelings, but it began to dawn on me that I could allow myself to feel physical discomfort but still be safe.

This opened a whole new world for me. Easing myself into reconnecting my mind and body allowed me to appreciate discomfort, focus through it instead of ignore it, and come out the other side with new strength. It empowered me by allowing me to feel the discomfort and be in control of whether I pushed on, easing further into the pose, or honoured myself by backing off to a more comfortable level.

I started experimenting with doing the same with my emotions. I began allowing myself to express my emotions, feel the vulnerability, but still feel safe. Of course, I had to find the right person to do this with, at first. It had to be someone I actually felt I could trust, someone I did not have to worry would cause me pain if I exposed this part of myself. My emotions began tumbling in, almost overwhelmingly so. I did not always know or understand how to deal with them, certainly not positively.

Eventually, I began to see my own strength. I saw first-hand I could be emotional, then recover. This allowed me to begin trusting myself. Trusting that I could handle different situations, emotions, discomfort, and still be safe. With trust and strength, comes power. I was gaining my power back.

If you have never practised yoga before, it is worth a try. I would recommend beginning by finding an instructor you feel comfortable with, rather than practising from the comfort of your own home before you are sure you are practising the poses correctly and safely.

I used to practise weekly, in a studio with an amazing yogi. Now I practise daily, bringing myself through a series of sun salutations every morning, in the comfort of my 'zen den', as I call it. There are many types of yoga, so I would recommend signing up for trial passes with several studios and/or instructors so you can try your hand at each style available to you, then decide which is the best fit.

For those of you who already know how incredibly empowering it feels to stand tall on your yoga mat, take a moment each time you practise to allow yourself to fully feel the pose. Let your mind rest on any of your muscles, and allow yourself to feel the discomfort, strength, or weakness that lies within, with no judgement, knowing you are safe.

If this is a new concept for you, start slow. Just focus once, on one area, each time you practise. Allow yourself time to build up your confidence. Let yourself feel what it is like to be safe while, at the same time, in some discomfort. You will soon see what I learned to see – you can have both. Use this new-found awareness to bridge the gap between your body and your mind, allowing the two to reconnect with love. You will also start to really feel your connection to your Higher Self, and the Universe through your yoga practice. This can also be said of meditation, which we will discuss next.

• Chapter 13 •

Strengthening Your Connection Through Meditation

The 'connection' I am referring to in this chapter is multifaceted. Meditation, along with many other modalities such as yoga, Reiki, chakra work, crystals, etc... can really strengthen your connection to yourself, your Higher Self, and to the Universe. By grounding and centring yourself in this way, you deepen your connection to others, to your work, and to your life in general. It allows clarity on your life's lessons and even your purpose. In doing so, meditation can bring about a true calmness you may have never felt before.

It is natural to spend the majority of our time 'in our heads'. Most of us talk to ourselves (I am sure that is not just me, right?) on a regular basis. Even when we are in conversation with others, there is usually an internal conversation going on that you are also managing. You know what I am talking about, I know you do. That moment when someone comes up and gives you a compliment and you smile, giving the polite response of 'thank you', while in your head you are gloating – to yourself – about how you were right to try on five outfits before settling on that one. There is also the conversation you will have with yourself about the time it took to do your hair or make-up. Then there is the even deeper conversation where you will ask yourself if you heard any hint of sarcasm in their voice – could they be mocking you instead of complimenting you? Why would they choose *that* to give you a compliment on? And so on, and so on.

We do it so often that we can catch ourselves missing an important part of a conversation because of our own internal one. How many times in one day do you find yourself having to ask someone to repeat themselves, pretending it is because you did not quite hear them? Or perhaps you are too embarrassed to ask yet again, so you try to put the pieces together by listening intently now – like if you have walked into a room midway through a conversation between others that you are trying to insert yourself into.

We are thinkers. Most of us are over-thinkers. And this can be a real problem, especially when we are trying to be connected to the Universe and Higher Self.

It is also a real problem for another reason. According to Dr Raj Raghunathan in *Psychology Today* (2013), up to 70% of our mental chatter is negative. 70%! So, if our day is filled with mental conversations we are aware of, and those we are not so aware of, and 70% of them are negative, what do you think that is doing to your connection to self?

Using the positive intentions and affirmations in our previous chapter is a great way to start changing the language you are using with yourself, along with yoga to help you experience healthy, safe discomfort, and now meditation. Meditation is designed to clear the mind chatter. When you think about meditation, I bet you think of someone sitting on a cushion on the floor, perfect posture, eyes closed, with no thoughts whatsoever in their brain. Just stillness, a sense of calm and peace washing over them.

The truth is, it can be very difficult to get to that point. More importantly, to have a successful meditation practice, you do not need to be perfect. When you first begin, you will probably be uncomfortable and your mind will constantly drift. I know when I first began adding meditation to my daily routine, I would sit on my cushion on the floor and catch my mind wandering constantly. I thought about my grocery list, what I was going to do immediately after I got up from the floor, how much my back hurt, how I wasn't doing it properly because I kept having these thoughts, and more and more judgement of how I was failing. That is totally not the point of meditation.

So I backed off a bit. I changed course. I did not give up, I just found an app to use to ease me into my meditation practice. Instead of listening to meditative music, I listen to guided meditations and visualisations. I let my brain focus on their words instead of my own. That allowed me to still have my brain thinking, without judging myself for thinking. After two weeks, I was finding my brain was skipping ahead – I had learned the routine of the guidance. I moved on to a different guided meditation app. And then I created some of my own. Finally, I tried the meditation music again to see if I could sit in stillness.

Here is what I realised... We are all on our own path, both in life and in meditation. It is okay for your brain to wander. When my brain wanders, I do not judge myself, I thank myself for bringing this to my attention. I then gently guide my brain back towards the music, with love.

For me, this shows acceptance and respect for where I am that day, every day. Each day is different. Some are easier than others. Some days I get completely lost in the meditation, sitting for thirty minutes. Other days I am squirming through five minutes. I allow myself to do what I need to do – to find balance and calmness in my own way. Because, for me, meditation is not about doing something like someone else does it. It is about loving and honouring yourself.

Before meditation, I did not realise how difficult I found it to truly relax and find calm. I also did not realise how uncomfortable it made me to seek that calmness. With each day, I learned more about myself, my needs, weaknesses and strengths. I learned to appreciate each of these in order to respect and love myself. Now I honour what I need, not just in meditation, but throughout my entire day, every day. That is the true skill I perfected through meditation.

• Chapter 14 •

Daily Reflection

One of the best methods I used to really influence changes in my life, to become the best version of myself, was daily self-reflection. This is because, like most people, I was not even aware of what I was doing – my actions or reactions. Yes, I implemented everything we have discussed in this book, focusing heavily on creating, or tuning into, my connection to Self and the Universe.

But the bottom line was, I could change my habits to include many different activities, such as yoga, meditation, and positive intentions and affirmations, but until I really took stock of who I was, I could not make any lasting change. It is that old saying, 'You cannot fix what you do not know is broken'.

Going through the process of forgiveness through recognising my true life lessons, and my abuser's significant role in the unveiling of them, was a huge step forward. Surrendering control and learning to trust in myself and the Universe was vital in my healing.

However, the single most powerful tool I used was self-reflection. This is what ultimately allowed me to see and understand what I was doing to meet my needs, including why I was reacting and acting the way I was. It allowed me to look at the person I was from all angles, and determine where I wished to make constructive edits.

I gained so much strength and power during this process. For every moment I felt guilt over the person I had become, I also gained tremendous knowledge and understanding, and ultimately, compassion, for who and why I was who I was. I realised a few small changes were all that were necessary in some areas of my life. Most importantly, I realised making those small adjustments acted as fuel to propel me closer to the more major shifts I was determined to make.

For example, my ultimate motivation was to shift into a positive mindset and finally ditch the negative self-talk. I wanted to seriously kick that negative mantra of mine, the one placed there by my abuser, to the kerb. It was not one task I needed to complete in order to achieve this goal. No, it seemed far more overwhelming than that. Because it was.

These thoughts had permeated my entire being. I lost myself in them. They governed every decision I made and even haunted my dreams. The thought of just replacing them with positive thoughts was laughable.

However, when I began to take a serious look at who I was, and why I was making decisions, including my actions and reactions (something we rarely 'think' about, but just do), I truly came to know and understand myself. I was able to accept, respect and love myself. The reason behind my urge to change myself shifted. Instead of hating certain traits, or wanting him out of my head, or wanting people to like me, I simply was ready to let go.

I let go of his words, his beliefs, his need to control and dominate me, because I no longer needed any of it. That was no longer my comfort zone. I was ready to spread my wings. My shifting journey became about honouring myself rather than hating myself.

And here is how I did it. At the end of every day, I sat down with my journal and I did some reflection on each of the following:

1. What I was grateful for
2. Why I was grateful for each
3. How did I act and react today?
4. What opportunities may have been presented?

Let us tackle each one separately.

What I was grateful for

I am sure you have heard of this – perhaps you have even practised it yourself. Right now, this is all over the internet, my website and social pages included. Sitting down and writing out all the things, people, experiences and opportunities you are grateful for each day allows your brain to start shifting to remember and focus on the positive in your life. This is obviously crucial if you are looking to shift your mindset into the positive.

It is not the same as pretending everything is rose-coloured. Absolutely not. Rather, it forces you to search out and find something, anything, positive from each situation. Eventually, you begin to start looking for the positive throughout your day, which will allow you to shift from your negative thoughts more quickly. This will soon lead to you recognising the positive *in the moment,* allowing you to refocus your energies *before* you even jump into your old negative mantra and thinking patterns. You are, in essence, reprogramming your neural pathways to search the situation for the positive, rather than assuming the negative. This allows you to start recognising that the people in your life and the events are all opportunities for you to learn and grow, and to support and teach.

So many people believe having a positive mindset means you cannot allow yourself to experience any negativity. That is simply not true. Rather, it is about honouring your feelings and thoughts, while finding your strength to pull yourself out from any situation. It is not that the negative thoughts should not ever be there, but what you do with them, that matters.

Successful people are given lemons all the time. They do not throw them away to break free from the obstacle. No. They turn those lemons into what? Yep, lemonade. Having a positive mindset is more about knowing that you will be okay, no matter what happens. In this sense, a positive mindset is about self-love, respect and strength. This process of writing out your gratitude is not about never seeing things as negative again. Rather, it is about taking the negative and turning it into a strength.

Your challenge is to begin by writing out three things, people and experiences you are grateful for every day. When you start finding that less challenging, up it to five. Eventually, push yourself to finding ten things, people and experiences to be grateful for every day. You can stop writing them out, only when you can spot ten throughout the day, as it unfolds. Moreover, you need to be able to also catch yourself in the negative mindset, and use your gratitude to shift into the positive.

I would like to point out here that I still write out, or say out loud, my gratitude lists every time I am challenged, or feel down and out. It is just a simple, yet lovely, way to pull myself back to my reality. How I *choose* to react to this experience is exactly that – a choice.

Why I am grateful

This step is self-explanatory. Writing out what you are grateful for is a wonderful way to start shifting your brain, training it to look for the positive in all situations. What makes this process even more effective is understanding *why* you are grateful for everything on your list. Why? Good question.

Taking the time to write out exactly what makes you grateful for each item on your list allows your brain to find real meaning in this process, and to understand how to interpret opportunities (which we will talk about later in this chapter). Rather than just listing each person, thing or experience you are grateful for today, add a layer of texture to it by including a simple sentence as to why.

For example, I am grateful for the opportunity to write this book *because...*

It is a healing journey for me also

It helps me practise what I preach

It allows me an outlet to express myself

It allows me to reach, and help, countless women (and men)

It allows me to get closer to my goal of raising the spiritual consciousness of millions of people all over the globe

It allows me to get closer to my goal of shedding the stigma of being abused

It is a means for me to break my silence

Now, I have suggested you begin with one reason; however, you can list as many reasons as you like (the more the merrier). You can also get as in-depth and specific as you like.

How did I act and react today?

We all have moments we wish we could take back. Whether it was an expression on our face, or words spoken out of frustration, we can all relate.

Sometimes, we do not understand why we cannot change these reactions. I believe it is because we do not fully understand them. Not that we do not understand that we are frustrated or upset in some way, but why this situation or person has brought out the feeling in us. More importantly, we do not understand what we are getting from reacting in this way. Once we understand what we are getting from them, we can figure out how to meet that need in a more productive way, for our Highest good.

The same is true with our actions. For example, I used to try not to take charge in a group setting, even though I am a very dominant personality who likes to be social, am good with people, enjoy hard work, and am an extrovert. I kept finding that I would kick myself later, chastising my lack of initiative when the group was forming. Why did I not raise my hand, throwing my name into the hat to be the leader? Why did I not contribute more during our brainstorming sessions? Why did I not step up to assist with problem-solving when the need arose?

At first, I thought the obvious – I was afraid of rejection. That may have had a part in it, for sure. But when I began to really reflect at the end of each day, over my actions and reactions, I realised one of the needs I was meeting by doing (or not doing, as in this case), was safety.

We all have needs we are striving to meet, as we discussed at the beginning of this book. That means we are all finding ways to meet those needs, in the moment. But without a strong understanding of what those needs are, and how we are going about meeting them, we look for quick fixes. I was not putting myself forward for leadership positions because I feared being rejected, but because I feared failure. I realised I believed I was a failure. By being in a leadership position, I believed I would fail, and so would the group. By allowing myself to sit in the shadows, I could meet my needs for safety *and success* – the group would be successful because I was not at the helm, and if it was not, I was just a small cog in the wheel so I would not be responsible.

But that was not true success, was it? Not playing into my strengths and allowing myself to 'be safe' meant that I was failing myself.

By sitting down and thinking through all my decisions each day – even the ones made in the heat of the moment, that do not feel like decisions at all – I began to understand the deeply-rooted belief systems I had in place that were at the heart of every move I made. I could then work on my belief systems (we discussed this in an earlier chapter), and plan for how I would like to act and react in the future. This is only really possible when you understand what is driving you to make the decision in the first place.

The plan is simple. You need to decide how you can meet your need in a way that serves your Highest good. The need *does not* need to change. Your method of meeting the need does. In my example, I did not need to stop needing to be safe and successful. Instead, I needed to work out for myself how I could meet those needs more effectively. In other words, how could I play to my strengths to meet those needs, rather than push myself into the background?

As you can see, this self-reflection activity is multifaceted. You need to:

Break down your actions and reactions for the day

Uncover why you acted and reacted this way (what need was being met)

List the deeply-rooted beliefs about yourself

Determine how you can meet the need in a way that serves your Highest good

Put a plan in place for how you want to act and react in the future

Rewrite the script for your beliefs (previous chapter)

What opportunities may have been presented?

Last in your self-reflection activity, you need to have a look at the different experiences you faced today, and determine if any could have been opportunities. You do not need to know what the opportunities are at this point. All you need to do is be open to the idea some of the people and experiences in your day came about as a means to offer you something. It could have been a chance to learn, grow, or heal in your own journey. It may have been a chance to teach or support someone else in their journey. We all come into each other's lives for a reason, big or small. We often never understand the reasons, simply because we are not looking at life this way. Even when we do not understand the meaning, we can acknowledge there is one.

In this self-reflection exercise, you can think about anything in your day that was challenging or put a smile on your face. Perhaps you ran into an old colleague unexpectedly, or an old friend popped up on Facebook. Maybe your boss spoke to you in a way that caused you to doubt yourself, or stirred your emotions. Perhaps you spent a little time helping someone else with something – giving advice, just being a shoulder for them, training them on a new system – anything, big or small. When we make a point to list these things, even when we do not know their purpose, we start to see meaning in all areas of our lives.

This exercise is the same as the gratitude journal. You will want to do this every day. You will eventually begin to realise that you are recognising opportunities in the moment. The goal is for you to begin to handle your viewpoint and reaction to these people and experiences differently, because you recognise the possibility in all your interactions. In the next chapter, we will talk about why this is so important.

• Chapter 15 •

Taking Opportunities

In the last chapter, we talked about reflecting daily on your actions, reactions and your experiences and situations throughout each day.

The exercise is three-fold. It offers you the opportunity to shift your mindset, to begin seeing the positive in situations that at first appear negative. There is also the opportunity to gain a deeper understanding of your needs, how you are meeting them, and how you could continue to meet them in a more positive way that serves your Highest good. Lastly is opportunity itself. You are looking to find events, situations, people, or emotions you could identify as possible opportunities, which essentially shifts your perspective.

When you begin to see all situations, events, people and even your emotional reactions to them as opportunities to learn, grow and heal (or teach, and help someone else to grow and heal), you tend to take those opportunities. Each time you take an opportunity, you gain confidence. Of course, with gained confidence, you are more likely to take more leaps, taking more opportunities. It is a never-ending cycle that fuels itself.

Before we jump in to do this, we need to take a step back. Think about an experience you had in the past.

It does not have to be something as traumatic as abuse. It could be something small, but that impacted you greatly at the time. Take a moment to recall the negativity you felt because of that experience. How did it impact you at the time?

Now, fast-forward. It can be any time in your life after that experience, even now. Using hindsight, can you see how certain things unfolded because of that experience? Are any of them positive? Earlier in the book, I gave the example of the fire that destroyed my office. I explained how life at work had been increasingly tumultuous, causing me great despair. The fire was devastating, but it gave me the opportunity to seek out a new office space, away from the people causing me grief. Once I was in the new office and attracting others to work with me who were vibrating with the same energy frequency, and clients who loved the new space and were telling all their friends, massively increasing my business and thus my reputation, I was able to see the true opportunity that fire gave me.

It did not feel positive at the time. In fact, it felt like my world was crashing down upon me. But it was exactly what I needed to force me to grab hold of this opportunity. I would not have left that office otherwise. The rent was cheap, we were in a good location, and I was working with my friends. I thought I had it all. There would have been zero reason to risk all that to branch out on my own, expanding my business. In fact, the thought never once crossed my mind.

Even after closing my expanded and thriving Wellness Centre, and changing careers entirely, I am certain that fire was one of the best things that could have happened in my life. Part of why I am here today, living in a different country, married, a stepmum, and with a business I adore, is because that fire forced an opportunity upon me, and I had the strength and courage to take it.

I had no idea where it would lead. If I had had a crystal ball and would have seen that I would not even be a massage therapist fifteen years later, I might not have bothered to leave the safety of the original office, despite the uncomfortable situations between myself and my colleagues. All I could see was that moment, and all the moments before. I made my decision based on the judgement I was placing on my current circumstances. Little did I know how great an impact it would have on my life and career.

And that is the point, is it not? We do not have all the information. We cannot. We make so many decisions every day that impact the course of our lives, that it would be impossible to 'see' into our future. Which future? The future that lays before us now, or the one before us twenty minutes ago? It is evolving. All we can do is make decisions based on the information we have *right now*.

Looking back at experiences that were uncomfortable in some way, and then admitting and recognising how that experience helped to get us to the next destination in our journey, builds our confidence with the experiences we are facing today. So, let us have a look.

Using the same exercise from the previous chapter, you can reflect upon experiences to determine what lessons may have been available to you, the beliefs you would have either generated or reinforced because of the experience, and what opportunities they afforded you, even if those opportunities seemed to take months or years to unfold.

For example, I was married in 2001 to a wonderful, supportive man. He was the first man I had a relationship with who I knew would always be faithful. He was kind and gentle and put me on a pedestal. That was the first time I had been treated with such respect, and I was twenty-six when we married.

Fast-forward six years to 2007 and we were separating. I had closed down my Wellness Centre to work from home and, within a few weeks, was left juggling how to be in a live-in separation and work from home without having any awkwardness for my clients. As you can imagine, it was a very difficult and confusing time.

Within a few months, I was planning to buy a property I could both live and work from, and take on a housemate, because I did not have the income to do otherwise. I had pared down my business clientele, since I no longer had the massive overhead of the Wellness Centre. I was determined to be focused on my clients rather than on running a clinic. In doing so, I was making great money from my previous situation – married with a double income. I made enough to contribute to the bills and put lots of money into savings. But to run a household and business on my own? Nope.

That is when I realised why I had been driven to close my Wellness Centre in the first place. I thought it had been to allow me to focus on my treatments, rather than running a six-roomed facility. However, I realised then if I had not closed the business to begin working from home, I would not have had the financial ability to separate from my husband. There was no way I could run the business at the scale it had been, and run a household on my own. Now I was perfectly positioned to work from home, and pay my bills, with a little extra coming in from a housemate.

Fast-forward another ten years, and I am happily married to my second husband, and a stepmum to his wonderful kids. Not only that, but I live in a different country, on a different continent, and have changed careers twice. I could break down any one of those life experiences in the same way. They started as being difficult, but opened the door to new possibilities. I can say with absolute certainty my separation and subsequent divorce was an opportunity to walk on the path that would lead me here, to this moment. Was it easy? No. Was it emotionally exhausting? Yes. Would I do it all over again, knowing now what lay ahead? You bet I would!

I can say the same thing about my abuse. Of course, if I could go back, I would want to have a 'normal' childhood.

I would not wish my experience on anyone, certainly not on myself, again. However, since I cannot change what happened, I can instead *choose* to look back on that ten-year experience and see the opportunity it presented me. I learned life lessons because of that experience. I crawled my way out of the deepest, darkest hole, found my strength, and learned to fall in love with myself. Honestly, I have no idea if I would be the same person I am today, without that experience. Would I be writing this book, for example? Would I be a speaker and coach?

I am fairly certain my mission to shed the stigma of being abused by breaking my silence would not exist without that experience, as this would not be my story, or my life. There is even no guarantee I would have learned my life lessons. So, now it is time for you to do the same.

Write down an experience, big or small, but make it one that evoked a negative reaction; something that caused difficulty in the moment, and perhaps for many moments. Add to it the lessons you learned and the beliefs you gained or that were reinforced because of this experience. Play out your life from that point, like a film playing in the cinema.

Can you start to see how that experience opened the door for other key moments in your life? Is it possible the experience happened, along with many others, to get you to where you are today? If so, then write out how you have benefited, or how life has changed in the positive, because of that experience.

Once you are able to see that past experiences were opportunities, you are more likely to allow yourself to see current experiences are also opportunities. This causes you to experience them differently, without the anger, frustration, sadness or being overwhelmed. Whatever the experience causes, you will start to see past it. You will not understand what opportunity it is giving necessarily, and you do not need to. All you need is to accept that it *is* an opportunity. Your viewpoint will change, and your relationship to the experience will also change. Most importantly, you will be on high alert for the opportunities themselves. This means you will be more likely to grab them. Each time you do, your confidence in yourself will grow, as will your perception of your circumstances. You will fight to see the positive; to make lemonade out of lemons.

• Chapter 16 •

How to Ensure Success When Setting Your Goals

Congratulations on getting through this book and all the amazing revelations you have had. Now it is time to make a plan. Understanding how energy works, the power of a positive mindset, the impact your beliefs are having on your life, and how your perception of your life lessons allows for forgiveness, is huge. Also, having so many tangible tools at your disposal to use to inspire change is empowering.

But, without a plan to actually use those tools, these are just words on paper. One of the major lessons I have learned in this life is how easy and enticing it is to believe that major changes will happen by just hoping it to be so. I once was someone who did everything I could to escape from the work necessary to make real and lasting change. I believed that by just reading a book and highlighting some sections that moved me, I would automatically apply those concepts to my life.

Guess what? It did not happen! No more than you reminding yourself tomorrow is garbage day and you need to put the bins out. They are not going to magically roll themselves out just because you had the thought. No more than someone magically appearing, excited to put them out on your behalf. You are going to have to put your coat and shoes on, walk out the door, and push, pull or drag those bins to the kerb. That is right. You, and only you, can do this work – and it is work.

According to many experts, it takes twenty-one to sixty-six days to create a new habit (or change an old one). Why the large discrepancy? Because there are many factors at play here. How long have you had the old habits? How entrenched are they? How much are you relying on them to meet your needs? Are you able to make the changes you are looking for, consistently every day? These are but a few questions you need to ask yourself, which will greatly impact the length of time you need to make consistent effort to promote the change you seek. For example, in the new year, everyone and their brother makes a resolution for the entire year, right? How long do they last? Most do not even last the first month. We all know this because we have had it happen to ourselves. We can relate to having the best of intentions to make a change.

But here is the problem, and it is three-fold:

Going too big

Many people start out with a huge change. If their goal is to be more fit and healthy, they plan to begin an *entirely* new diet and exercise regime on January 1st. Of course, they forgot they would likely be tired and hung over from New Year's Eve the night before, so they either ditch day one or do not put in full effort because they do not feel their best. Instead of easing themselves into their new programme, they are too keen and set themselves up for failure. Very quickly, the expectation of transforming their diet and working out X number of days a week becomes unmanageable.

They need to be consistent, which means doing this every day for twenty-one days, for this to become the new habit. They are not going to work out every day for twenty-one days. Everyone knows their body needs to rest so it can repair itself. So, for every day of rest, they are in essence being inconsistent. Twenty-one days now starts creeping into thirty days and beyond.

On top of this, many people who make such a radical change in their routine, such as with their diet, will offset this with 'cheat days'. These are days when they allow themselves to eat whatever they want and, of course, not exercise. Again, this pushes the twenty-one days well beyond, into the thirty and forty-day mark. Most diets out there are far shorter than this. This is one of the many reasons that most experts advocate a healthy *lifestyle* change, rather than an actual diet. This means you make sensible changes to your eating habits for life, rather than a short period.

So, rather than transforming your entire diet, you start with smaller portion sizes. When that feels normal, you add some more vegetables. You then extend this to cut out certain foods, or at least limit the amount you have of these foods, like sweets. Next, you change your snack foods to a healthier option. Yes, generally speaking this will take much longer to get to the point where your entire diet is perfectly healthy, but you will be gaining many rewards, and will find your version of a balanced and healthy diet, making it much more likely you will stick with it. After all, you are not trying to diet for a specific period of time, you are changing your eating lifestyle forever.

The exact same can be said here with shifting your mindset and challenging your self-limiting beliefs to build the life you truly deserve. Rather than this being a diet that only lasts a small portion of time, it needs to be a lifestyle change implemented consistently over the course of time.

Unrealistic expectations

The second area people go wrong, despite their best intentions, is with the unrealistic expectations they place on themselves. I do not mean the goal of losing X number of pounds, or becoming healthier, is unrealistic. Rather, the means they choose to go about reaching that goal is unrealistic.

For example, many people vow to join the gym in January as part of their resolution to get fitter. Excellent, except for one problem: They do not have any time in the day to go to the gym. This results in them either never following through and paying for a membership they never use, or they schedule in an unrealistic gym date they simply cannot meet day in and day out. How many times have you heard someone say they have joined the gym and are going to get up at 5am so they have time to work out before work? Or they will go to the gym late at night after they put the kids to bed?

Many people know this is unrealistic, so they will opt to work out from home, reducing the driving time to the gym and back. Are they able to keep up with that routine? Nope. Why not? Because they 'forgot' to factor in how exhausted they normally are at the end of the day, or how they do not function first thing in the morning. Yes, they are hoping they will have more energy because of working out, but they neglected to factor in the time it would take for them to start feeling those benefits. Again, it takes a minimum of twenty-one days of *consistency* to instil a new habit. Factor in the rest days they will need, along with all the times life just gets in the way, and they are easily creeping in on the maximum of sixty-six days to change that habit. How likely are they to continue this new plan of theirs for that long?

Again, the goal should not be to work out for a certain period of time, but to create a healthy lifestyle change. The goal therefore needs to be tangible. It may take longer to reach by starting slower, but to truly be healthier, this needs to be maintainable.

Like the diet example, so many people think they have to hit a new workout regime hard. However, small and gradual changes in your lifestyle lead to more long-term gains because you are more likely to implement an actual healthy lifestyle that lasts versus a short-term workout goal.

For example, if you are not someone who particularly enjoys hard workouts, why are you starting your goal or resolution by joining a gym and taking all their difficult workout classes, never mind doing this at some unreasonable hour of the day? You could start slower. If you are not someone who goes out for walks, your body will view walking as exercise. So, begin by incorporating more walking in your day – take the stairs instead of the lift or escalator; make time for a fifteen-minute walk on your lunch break. When that begins to feel normal, like part of your routine, then buy or borrow ankle or wrist weights to wear during your walk. Then, increase your walking pace. Start extending this to adding some star jumps or burpees at the end of your walk, after your muscles have warmed up. This way, not only are you making the workouts themselves more reasonable, but also the amount of time you need to invest.

Using part of your lunch hour is much more reasonable than expecting yourself to wake up ready for a hard workout at 5am. Again, the aim is to make a lifestyle change, forever.

This too is the perfect analogy for the work I will be challenging you with through the thirty-day challenge at the end of this book. We are looking for a lifestyle change that allows for a long-term, palpable change in your life.

Beliefs

There are reasons people do this, essentially sabotaging their attempt to reach their goals. Have you guessed the main reason yet? Yep, it is their deeply-rooted, self-limiting beliefs about themselves, what they are capable of and what they deserve. Now you have read this book you have a greater understanding of how their beliefs would cause them to go down this road: They do not believe they can do it, and they do not believe they are worthy of success.

But having this goal also meets a need, whatever that might be. Perhaps they feel if they become fit and healthy, they will have positive attention, acceptance and love. Whatever it is, they feel they do not have it now, and by achieving this goal, they will. Because this is something they truly want, they set the goal but, because of their beliefs, they will never *allow* themselves to reach the goal.

The same is true for those who set the goal then wait for someone else to magically do all the work for them so they can reap the reward without any of the hardships. These are people who set goals that are nearly impossible to gauge, like: 'I'm going to be nicer to myself and others'. What does that even look like? They have set themselves up for failure because they have not outlined any tangible ways to implement the goal or assess themselves.

In this case, the person never attempts to attain their goal. Rather, setting the goal meets their need, and the fact it is impossible to assess their success takes the pressure off. Now they do not feel any guilt if they fail because there is literally no way of showing either has happened.

Why have I used this diet and exercise example seemingly out of nowhere? Because just about everyone can relate, at some point in their lives, to setting a goal similar to this.

There is method to my madness. Of course, this concept applies to everything we have discussed in this book. You have to be willing to do the work. You cannot expect anyone else will do any of this work for you – not because there is not anyone out there who would love and care for you enough to do it, but because no one else can. It is not enough to read this book and have the revelations. You might have even highlighted some sections – great. It is still not going to magically happen. *You* are going to have implement the strategies we discussed throughout this book to make the changes you are looking for.

And mark my words, if you attempt these strategies like the diet and exercise resolution we just discussed, you will not get to day twenty-one, never mind sixty-six. You will have long given up on, and perhaps even forgotten, your goal by then.

The plan

1. *Be specific*

If you learned anything from our diet and exercise example, I am hoping it is that you need to break down your larger, ultimate goal, into manageable and tangible tasks.

For example, let us say the ultimate goal is to change into a healthy, confident, empowered person who leaves their past in the past, lives fully in the present, and builds the life they truly deserve. That is great. How are you going to assess your success? None of these ambitions will be easily assessed, just like the 'I am going to be nicer to myself and others' target. Start off with understanding your ultimate outcome, and then get specific. Think about how you will be able to tell if you have achieved your goal.

For example, with our goal, I would break down the large goal into smaller, more specific chunks: In this case, to be confident. How will you tell if you have become confident? Is there a situation you typically find yourself in where you lack confidence? Could you be specific about which situations you will be in where you will feel confident? That way, when you find yourself in that situation, you know this is an opportunity to apply whatever strategies you have, and assess your success by how confident you feel in comparison to before you began.

2. *Start small*

Like with our diet and exercise example, if you 'go all in' right from the beginning, you are likely going to set unrealistic expectations.

So, start out small. Begin with one thing you can do to work towards your specific goal, not twenty-five things. Keep it simple and tangible, something you will actually be able to have time for and might enjoy. If you have something in mind, but you know it will take more time than you have, or will push you outside your comfort zone, break it down further.

For example, if you have decided that to be more confident you need to put yourself in more situations where you can demonstrate your skills, not just for the higher powers in your organisation, but for yourself, then you are very likely to show yourself, and them, your skillset and get praise. However, if this is a big leap outside your comfort zone, you are also likely to cause yourself great stress and anxiety, which will either impede your success or your perception of it. In essence, you will be so focused on how anxious you were that you will not allow yourself to hear and feel the praises sung to you.

Instead of having to present at a big meeting, make arrangements to present to far fewer people. If there is no opportunity to do this at work, get your friends, family and neighbours involved. Invite them over for a coffee, or wine, and give them your presentation. When that goes well, invite a few more and do the same. Each experience will allow you to build your confidence without having the risk of presenting in front of your managers or boss. Once your confidence is higher, the thought of making the larger presentation will not be as anxiety-filled.

3. *Repetition is key*

As you are adding in tasks to help you reach your goals, repetition is key. As we already discussed, it takes twenty-one to sixty-six days to create a new habit, or replace an old one. It does not matter what the habit is; consistency is key to your success. That means that implementing my example for increasing confidence will work beautifully for that presentation but, if you stop there, your confidence will most certainly plummet.

You need to continue to push yourself to increase your confidence, rather than perceiving the goal to be met and moving on. What you will find then is the next time you feel a lack of confidence, you will chastise me, this book, and my strategy (anyone but yourself), because you will fail to see the connection between your lack of consistency and your lack of confidence.

4. ***Build upon your tasks each day***

Like all of us, you most certainly have many changes you are eager to implement, many goals to set. As you will see at the end of this chapter, building upon your tasks each day helps to push yourself forward. For example, if you want to learn to meditate, you would not start out with a ninety-minute silent meditation, would you? You would probably search for an introductory guided meditation series to ease your way in. But you also would not do one introductory session and replay that over and over again for the rest of your life, would you?

I am guessing you would progress through the introductory series until you felt comfortable enough, and then would branch out in search of other guided meditations. You might eventually begin searching for unguided meditation music as well. Certainly, you would stretch far enough to increase the length of your meditations, even if only by a few minutes. You would effectively build upon your meditation, at your own pace, until you reached the perfect mix of duration, music and guidance. At that point, you might choose to meditate daily, or even several times a day.

In this way, building upon your tasks gets you from where you are now (no experience), to where you want to be (daily meditation for fifteen minutes), in a gentle yet concise way that will leave you more likely to continue your meditation practice for years to come. The same is true for any other goal, such as building your confidence, or shifting your mindset from that of a survivor to that of a warrior.

I have designed a system which I use in my coaching programme, online courses, workshops, and even in my speeches, including the tactics I spoke of throughout the book. I have also used simple tasks that worked for me in transforming my life. In this, our final chapter, I will now introduce you to, and walk you through, your Thirty-Day Challenge.

Your Challenge

After all your reading and all the subsequent revelations, you now have a choice: Do nothing and expect nothing better in your life; or do the work you need to do to transform your life.

A dear friend of mine, Katie McClelland, who has survived drug addiction and works to help others grow and heal in their own right, has a fantastic expression about the stages you need to go through before you are ready to do the work: Do you HAVE to, are you WILLING to, or do you WANT to? Speaking from personal experience, you begin by feeling like you have to do the work. This may be because someone else tells you they have had enough and threatens to leave if you do not get help, or because you have reached a point where you realise if you do not heal, life will not change.

Unfortunately, that does not mean you are ready. In fact, this is when you are least likely to invest in the work you need to do. Instead, you may go to rehab, start seeing a therapist, or even hire a coach so you can tell yourself, and others, you are getting help. Really, you are just there, not participating, waiting for someone else to save you and make this all go away.

The next stage is recognising you are willing to do the work. This stage causes you to actually seek out help in the form of support groups, a therapist or coach, or even deep soul-searching by reading books on the matter.

Instead of just turning up at your therapy or coaching sessions, you are more interactive and do one or two of the exercises suggested to you. If this is where you are at right now, you probably tried one or two of the suggested tasks within this book. Not all of them, but a couple.

Guess what? You are still not actually ready to do the work. Nope. Even when you are willing, you will convince yourself that you *are* doing the work – after all, you have bought all the books and are going to therapy, doing a few tasks here and there. Really, you are still looking for someone else to do the work for you, whether it be the book, group, members in the group, therapist, coach, rehab clinic, your family or friends. Anyone but *you*. Not until you reach the final stage where you want to change your ways to transform your life, will you actually start doing the real work.

See the difference there? You start by realising you have to do it, then move into being willing to do it (but not *actually* fully doing it), to finally wanting to do the work.

Where are you on this spectrum? If you are brutally honest with yourself and you realise you feel you have to or are willing to, then this is where our journey together ends. That is, until you want to move forward. Once you reach that point, come on back. Have another read of the book and continue on with the challenge I am about to unfold for you here.

There are no hard feelings. Everyone is exactly where they need to be on their path. You need to honour that, because I do. You have gone far enough to not just purchase this book, but you have read it as well. That is a great sign that you are moving in the right direction. Do not push yourself faster or farther than you are ready in this moment. You have to truly want it, and that includes wanting to do the work to transform into the person you deserve to be. Until then, take the time you need.

If you are wanting this, and you are excited about facing a challenge that will really get you shifting your perspective and changing the way you experience your life, keep on reading. Your Thirty-Day Challenge begins today.

I have created a schedule of activities for you, with everything we have spoken about in this book. Not only does it provide you with space to write in, but it also prompts you for meditations. To officially register for this free challenge, and download your own useable copy of the workbook, please visit www.lifelikeyoumeanit.com/new-year-new-you. You will receive a new email daily with links to download my suggested meditations. If you are comfortable with meditation and have music or guided meditations you enjoy using, then please do. Keep in mind that I have suggested very specific meditations to support you in your work, as I anticipate certain tasks within this challenge will cause you to need to surrender control, release your fears, forgive, protect yourself with white light, etc.

You will also notice that there is a tick list for each day. That is because this challenge builds upon itself each day. Rather than replacing one activity with another, you are encouraged to add each challenge into your repertoire. This is because of what we spoke of earlier in the chapter – we want to set you up for success! Rather than starting so big that you cannot keep up, or requiring you to spend hours a day you do not have, ultimately setting you up for failure, we will gradually build upon each day.

The key to this challenge, of course, is repetition. You need to show up each day, for thirty days, so you have the best chance of setting new habits and replacing old ones. Some tasks are specifically at the start of the day, while others are at the end. I suggest you read ahead to see what is required of you so you can schedule in your time when it best suits you. For example, if the evening is really the only time you will feasibly be able to spare, you can use the evening to set the following day's positive intentions. You will need to repeat them in your head while getting ready in the morning, but the work to brainstorm what will work best for you on any given day can be done the night before. While you will come across the occasional challenge only required on that day, the rest are designed to be repeated day in and day out. You may find that some of the one-time-only challenges are a little more complex. If this is your finding, feel free to take a few days to complete it, as long as you continue with the rest of the challenge simultaneously.

I hope you enjoy your challenge, and find it includes everything we discussed throughout this book, leading the way for a serious shift in your mindset and how you perceive your experience of life. You had no control over what happened then, but you are the only one with control over how you allow that experience to influence your life today. Remember, your needs do not need changing, just the way you are going about meeting them.

I will leave you with my favourite quote; the quote that really hit home for me and caused me to shift from willing to wanting: 'She needed a hero, so that is what she became'.

The Thirty-Day Challenge

DAY ONE:

Meditation

Let us begin gently by finding ten minutes of time for yourself today. Finding time for yourself can be a lot harder than it sounds, which is why we are starting off small and tangible. You deserve this; you are worth the time. Before you begin to tell yourself all the reasons you do not have ten minutes today, remember that if your car breaks down, you will find the time to repair it. Better yet, you make the time to bring it in for regular maintenance so it does not break down, right? Enough said!

We really are starting small and tangible with a beautiful 'Higher Self' meditation that is just four minutes. If you have never tried meditation before, this is a gentle introduction. If you have more experience, you will find the visualisation very appealing.

It does not matter what time of day you practise this meditation, nor does it matter how often. If you resonate with this, you are welcome to include it in your daily routine whenever it suits. And, at under four minutes, you will hardly notice the time it has taken from your day.

Again, the link to formally register for this free challenge and get access to your workbook and all the meditations is: www.lifelikeyoumeanit.com/new-year-new-you

Please recycle any of the meditations that you resonate with on days when a new meditation is not provided. Enjoy!

Checklist:

- ☐ Meditated

Day two:

Replacing Negative Thoughts

Today involves you recognising any negative thoughts you have, about yourself or others, and discovering the cause. Finally, you will replace these thoughts with their positive counterpart. As time goes on, look for a pattern in how you are reacting in certain situations.

There is also a lovely meditation for today called 'White Light Protection'. Enjoy!

Negative Thought	Cause	Replacement Thought

Checklist:

- ☐ Meditated
- ☐ Replaced negative thoughts

DAY THREE:

Meditation

You have made it to day three!

This is a new meditation today called 'Happiness'.

Remember to also continue with replacing your negative thoughts throughout your day.

Enjoy!

Negative Thought	Cause	Replacement Thought

Checklist:

- ☐ Meditated
- ☐ Replaced negative thoughts

Day four:

Gratitude

One of the greatest ways to shift your mindset into the positive is to start looking for the positive. This will cause you to eventually see the positive as it occurs, throughout your day, which will cause you to look for it because you expect it. Such a simple exercise, yet so effective.

Enjoy!

Three things/people/experiences I am grateful for today:

1. ______________________________
2. ______________________________
3. ______________________________

Negative Thought	Cause	Replacement Thought

Checklist:

- ☐ Meditated
- ☐ Replaced negative thoughts
- ☐ Gratitude list

Day five:

Surrendering Control

One of the many things that fuels our behaviour is fear. Most times, fear is driven by a sense of having a lack of control. The problem is, we cannot control other people, most situations or experiences, and we certainly cannot control the past. The only control we really have is within. We can control ourselves, our reactions to others, our reactions to situations and experiences. Everything else, we either cause great anxiety by attempting to control the uncontrollable, or we surrender the need to control.

Write in your experience and get real about whether or not you had/have any control. If not, surrender. Enjoy!

Experience	Can you control this?

Three things/people/experiences I am grateful for today:

1. ______________________________

2. ______________________________

3. ______________________________

Negative Thought	Cause	Replacement Thought

Checklist:

- ☐ Meditated
- ☐ Replaced negative thoughts
- ☐ Gratitude list

Day six: ____

Positive Intentions

Set three positive intentions today. They must be positive, focusing on what you want, not on what you do not want. Think about these intentions as you get ready in the morning, and bring them back up in your mind throughout the day when needed. Enjoy!

My positive intentions for today are:

1. ______________________________
2. ______________________________
3. ______________________________

Three things/people/experiences I am grateful for today:

1. ______________________________
2. ______________________________
3. ______________________________

Negative Thought	Cause	Replacement Thought

Checklist:

- ☐ Meditated
- ☐ Replaced negative thoughts
- ☐ Gratitude list
- ☐ Set positive intentions

Day seven:

Meditation

Today includes a beautiful 'Forgiveness' meditation. You can use this to help you on your journey by applying forgiveness to anyone, including yourself. Enjoy!

My positive intentions for today are:

1. ______
2. ______
3. ______

Three things/people/experiences I am grateful for today:

1. ______
2. ______
3. ______

Negative Thought	Cause	Replacement Thought

Checklist:

- ☐ Meditated
- ☐ Replaced negative thoughts
- ☐ Gratitude list
- ☐ Set positive intentions

Day eight:

Daily Reactions Self-Reflection

Reflect today on any reaction you had that was at first negative. This can be internally (self-talk), or external. What did you gain from this? What basic needs did you meet (to be safe, accepted, loved...). Finally, is there an alternative way you can react in the future and still meet the need? Enjoy!

My positive intentions for today are:

1. ______________________________
2. ______________________________
3. ______________________________

Three things/people/experiences I am grateful for today:

1. ______________________________
2. ______________________________
3. ______________________________

Replacing Negative Thoughts

Negative Thought	Cause	Replacement Thought

Daily Reactions Self-Reflection

Reaction	What did you gain from reacting this way?	What needs were met?	Alternative way

Checklist:

- ☐ Meditated
- ☐ Replaced negative thoughts
- ☐ Gratitude list
- ☐ Set positive intentions
- ☐ Self-reflection

DAY NINE: ______

Meditation

Today's challenge involves a 'Releasing Fears' meditation. Enjoy!

My positive intentions for today are:

1. ______
2. ______
3. ______

Three things/people/experiences I am grateful for today:

1. ______
2. ______
3. ______

Replacing Negative Thoughts

Negative Thought	Cause	Replacement Thought

Daily Reactions Self-Reflection

Reaction	What did you gain from reacting this way?	What needs were met?	Alternative way

Checklist:

- ☐ Meditated
- ☐ Replaced negative thoughts
- ☐ Gratitude list
- ☐ Set positive intentions
- ☐ Self-reflection

Day ten: ____________________

Expanded Gratitude List

Today we are simply expanding your gratitude list. You are now challenged to find ten things/people/experiences you are grateful for each day. Enjoy!

My positive intentions for today are:

1. ____________________
2. ____________________
3. ____________________

Ten things/people/experiences I am grateful for today:

1. ____________________
2. ____________________
3. ____________________
4. ____________________
5. ____________________
6. ____________________
7. ____________________
8. ____________________
9. ____________________
10. ____________________

Replacing Negative Thoughts

Negative Thought	Cause	Replacement Thought

Daily Reactions Self-Reflection

Reaction	What did you gain from reacting this way?	What needs were met?	Alternative way

Checklist:

- ☐ Meditated
- ☐ Replaced negative thoughts
- ☐ Gratitude list
- ☐ Set positive intentions
- ☐ Self-reflection

DAY ELEVEN: ______________________________________

Meditation

Today's meditation is a glorious 'Healing, Protection' meditation. Enjoy!

My positive intentions for today are:

1. ______________________________________
2. ______________________________________
3. ______________________________________

Ten things/people/experiences I am grateful for today:

1. ______________________________________
2. ______________________________________
3. ______________________________________
4. ______________________________________
5. ______________________________________
6. ______________________________________
7. ______________________________________
8. ______________________________________
9. ______________________________________
10. ______________________________________

Replacing Negative Thoughts

Negative Thought	Cause	Replacement Thought

Daily Reactions Self-Reflection

Reaction	What did you gain from reacting this way?	What needs were met?	Alternative way

Checklist:

- ☐ Meditated
- ☐ Replaced negative thoughts
- ☐ Gratitude list
- ☐ Set positive intentions
- ☐ Self-reflection

DAY TWELVE:

Shifting Old Belief Patterns

Today we are looking at shifting your old belief patterns by first identifying the original belief you gained from an experience, and then the actual reality, or truth. Take the time to look at each belief, and search for the reality. You have likely found 'evidence' to support this belief, but that was just what you were *choosing* to see. What is the real truth? Enjoy!

My positive intentions for today are:

1. ______
2. ______
3. ______

Ten things/people/experiences I am grateful for today:

1. ______
2. ______
3. ______
4. ______
5. ______
6. ______
7. ______
8. ______
9. ______
10. ______

Replacing Negative Thoughts

Negative Thought	Cause	Replacement Thought

Daily Reactions Self-Reflection

Reaction	What did you gain from reacting this way?	What needs were met?	Alternative way

Shifting Old Belief Patterns

Experience	Original Belief	Reality/Truth

Checklist:

- ☐ Meditated
- ☐ Replaced negative thoughts
- ☐ Gratitude list
- ☐ Set positive intentions
- ☐ Self-reflection

Day thirteen:

Meditation

Today's meditation is designed to support you with yesterday's challenge, shifting your beliefs. It is called, 'The Beach' Meditation. Enjoy!

My positive intentions for today are:

1. ________________________________
2. ________________________________
3. ________________________________

Ten things/people/experiences I am grateful for today:

1. ________________________________
2. ________________________________
3. ________________________________
4. ________________________________
5. ________________________________
6. ________________________________
7. ________________________________
8. ________________________________
9. ________________________________
10. ________________________________

Replacing Negative Thoughts

Negative Thought	Cause	Replacement Thought

Daily Reactions Self-Reflection

Reaction	What did you gain from reacting this way?	What needs were met?	Alternative way

Checklist:

- ☐ Meditated
- ☐ Replaced negative thoughts
- ☐ Gratitude list
- ☐ Set positive intentions
- ☐ Self-reflection

Day fourteen: ____________________

Deserve List

Today's challenge is all about looking at what you deserve in all aspects of your life. The objective is not to focus on how you will attain these things, rather on what you actually deserve, plain and simple.

My positive intentions for today are:

1. ____________________
2. ____________________
3. ____________________

Ten things/people/experiences I am grateful for today:

1. ____________________
2. ____________________
3. ____________________
4. ____________________
5. ____________________
6. ____________________
7. ____________________
8. ____________________
9. ____________________
10. ____________________

Replacing Negative Thoughts

Negative Thought	Cause	Replacement Thought

Daily Reactions Self-Reflection

Reaction	What did you gain from reacting this way?	What needs were met?	Alternative way

What I Deserve *(we'll go back to this list and add to it each day)*

Health	Wealth	Career	Personal

Checklist:

- ☐ Meditated
- ☐ Replaced negative thoughts
- ☐ Gratitude list
- ☐ Set positive intentions
- ☐ Self-reflection
- ☐ Deserve list

Day fifteen:

Meditation

Today's meditation works beautifully with the work you began yesterday – what you deserve. From this point forward, you are to add to your deserve list each day by adding a few more items to your list from yesterday. Enjoy!

My positive intentions for today are:

1. ______________________________
2. ______________________________
3. ______________________________

Ten things/people/experiences I am grateful for today:

1. ______________________________
2. ______________________________
3. ______________________________
4. ______________________________
5. ______________________________
6. ______________________________
7. ______________________________
8. ______________________________
9. ______________________________
10. ______________________________

Replacing Negative Thoughts

Negative Thought	Cause	Replacement Thought

Daily Reactions Self-Reflection

Reaction	What did you gain from reacting this way?	What needs were met?	Alternative way

Checklist:

- ☐ Meditated
- ☐ Replaced negative thoughts
- ☐ Gratitude list
- ☐ Set positive intentions
- ☐ Self-reflection
- ☐ Deserve list

Day sixteen:

Vision Board

Today's challenge is to create a vision board based on your deserve list. Just cut out some pictures that represent what you deserve, and paste them on to paper. Place it somewhere you will see it every day to reinforce your goals. Enjoy!

My positive intentions for today are:

1. ____________________
2. ____________________
3. ____________________

Ten things/people/experiences I am grateful for today:

1. ____________________
2. ____________________
3. ____________________
4. ____________________
5. ____________________
6. ____________________
7. ____________________
8. ____________________
9. ____________________
10. ____________________

Replacing Negative Thoughts

Negative Thought	Cause	Replacement Thought

Daily Reactions Self-Reflection

Reaction	What did you gain from reacting this way?	What needs were met?	Alternative way

Checklist:

- ☐ Meditated
- ☐ Replaced negative thoughts
- ☐ Gratitude list
- ☐ Set positive intentions
- ☐ Self-reflection
- ☐ Deserve list

Day seventeen:

Meditation

Today's meditation is about turning your dreams to reality – fitting, right? Enjoy!

My positive intentions for today are:

1. ____________________

2. ____________________

3. ____________________

Ten things/people/experiences I am grateful for today:

1. ____________________

2. ____________________

3. ____________________

4. ____________________

5. ____________________

6. ____________________

7. ____________________

8. ____________________

9. ____________________

10. ____________________

Replacing Negative Thoughts

Negative Thought	Cause	Replacement Thought

Daily Reactions Self-Reflection

Reaction	What did you gain from reacting this way?	What needs were met?	Alternative way

Checklist:

- ☐ Meditated
- ☐ Replaced negative thoughts
- ☐ Gratitude list
- ☐ Set positive intentions
- ☐ Self-reflection
- ☐ Deserve list

Day eighteen:

Meditation

We have another gorgeous meditation today to reinforce your deserve list, called 'Future Self'. Enjoy!

My positive intentions for today are:

1. ______________________________
2. ______________________________
3. ______________________________

Ten things/people/experiences I am grateful for today:

1. ______________________________
2. ______________________________
3. ______________________________
4. ______________________________
5. ______________________________
6. ______________________________
7. ______________________________
8. ______________________________
9. ______________________________
10. ______________________________

Replacing Negative Thoughts

Negative Thought	Cause	Replacement Thought

Daily Reactions Self-Reflection

Reaction	What did you gain from reacting this way?	What needs were met?	Alternative way

Checklist:

- ☐ Meditated
- ☐ Replaced negative thoughts
- ☐ Gratitude list
- ☐ Set positive intentions
- ☐ Self-reflection
- ☐ Deserve list

Day nineteen: ______________________________

Looking for Opportunities

Today's challenge allows you to begin to change your perspective on certain experiences in your life, shifting to see not just the positive, but the opportunity it has (or will) provide you. List the experience and then look for any positives that came out of that experience. Enjoy!

My positive intentions for today are:

1. ______________________________
2. ______________________________
3. ______________________________

Ten things/people/experiences I am grateful for today:

1. ______________________________
2. ______________________________
3. ______________________________
4. ______________________________
5. ______________________________
6. ______________________________
7. ______________________________
8. ______________________________
9. ______________________________
10. ______________________________

Replacing Negative Thoughts

Negative Thought	Cause	Replacement Thought

Daily Reactions Self-Reflection

Reaction	What did you gain from reacting this way?	What needs were met?	Alternative way

Looking for Opportunities

Experience	Opportunity

Checklist:

- ☐ Meditated
- ☐ Replaced negative thoughts
- ☐ Gratitude list
- ☐ Set positive intentions
- ☐ Self-reflection
- ☐ Deserve list
- ☐ Opportunities

Day twenty:

Meditation

Today's meditation is all about 'Releasing'. Let go of whatever you are holding. Enjoy!

My positive intentions for today are:

1. ______________________________
2. ______________________________
3. ______________________________

Ten things/people/experiences I am grateful for today:

1. ______________________________
2. ______________________________
3. ______________________________
4. ______________________________
5. ______________________________
6. ______________________________
7. ______________________________
8. ______________________________
9. ______________________________
10. ______________________________

Replacing Negative Thoughts

Negative Thought	Cause	Replacement Thought

Daily Reactions Self-Reflection

Reaction	What did you gain from reacting this way?	What needs were met?	Alternative way

Looking for Opportunities

Experience	Opportunity

Checklist:

- ☐ Meditated
- ☐ Replaced negative thoughts
- ☐ Gratitude list
- ☐ Set positive intentions
- ☐ Self-reflection
- ☐ Deserve list
- ☐ Opportunities

Day twenty-one:

Chakra Meditation

Chakras are energy centres in the body where energy flows. Today's challenge is to use the meditation provided to visualise colours which will balance your chakras. Enjoy!

My positive intentions for today are:

1. ____________________
2. ____________________
3. ____________________

Ten things/people/experiences I am grateful for today:

1. ____________________
2. ____________________
3. ____________________
4. ____________________
5. ____________________
6. ____________________
7. ____________________
8. ____________________
9. ____________________
10. ____________________

Replacing Negative Thoughts

Negative Thought	Cause	Replacement Thought

Daily Reactions Self-Reflection

Reaction	What did you gain from reacting this way?	What needs were met?	Alternative way

Looking for Opportunities

Experience	Opportunity

Checklist:

- ☐ Meditated
- ☐ Replaced negative thoughts
- ☐ Gratitude list
- ☐ Set positive intentions
- ☐ Self-reflection
- ☐ Deserve list
- ☐ Opportunities

Day twenty-two: ______________________________

Self-Care (Time)

Taking time for yourself each day teaches that you are worth taking that time. It causes you to believe you have value and worth, which is a game-changer. Take a little extra time for yourself today to do anything you want. Enjoy!

My positive intentions for today are:

1. ______________________________
2. ______________________________
3. ______________________________

Ten things/people/experiences I am grateful for today:

1. ______________________________
2. ______________________________
3. ______________________________
4. ______________________________
5. ______________________________
6. ______________________________
7. ______________________________
8. ______________________________
9. ______________________________
10. ______________________________

Replacing Negative Thoughts

Negative Thought	Cause	Replacement Thought

Daily Reactions Self-Reflection

Reaction	What did you gain from reacting this way?	What needs were met?	Alternative way

Looking for Opportunities

Experience	Opportunity

Checklist:

- ☐ Meditated
- ☐ Replaced negative thoughts
- ☐ Gratitude list
- ☐ Set positive intentions
- ☐ Self-reflection
- ☐ Deserve list
- ☐ Opportunities
- ☐ Self-care

Day twenty-three:

Meditation

Today's meditation is 'Healing Heart'. Enjoy!

My positive intentions for today are:

1. ____________________
2. ____________________
3. ____________________

Ten things/people/experiences I am grateful for today:

1. ____________________
2. ____________________
3. ____________________
4. ____________________
5. ____________________
6. ____________________
7. ____________________
8. ____________________
9. ____________________
10. ____________________

Replacing Negative Thoughts

Negative Thought	Cause	Replacement Thought

Daily Reactions Self-Reflection

Reaction	What did you gain from reacting this way?	What needs were met?	Alternative way

Looking for Opportunities

Experience	Opportunity

Checklist:

- ☐ Meditated
- ☐ Replaced negative thoughts
- ☐ Gratitude list
- ☐ Set positive intentions
- ☐ Self-reflection
- ☐ Deserve list
- ☐ Opportunities
- ☐ Self-care

DAY TWENTY-FOUR:

Self-Care (Eating Well)

Taking time for yourself teaches you how valuable and worthy you are. When you put healthy food into your body, you reinforce this lesson multi-fold. Begin adding a healthy snack in your day. Enjoy!

My positive intentions for today are:

1. ______
2. ______
3. ______

Ten things/people/experiences I am grateful for today:

1. ______
2. ______
3. ______
4. ______
5. ______
6. ______
7. ______
8. ______
9. ______
10. ______

Replacing Negative Thoughts

Negative Thought	Cause	Replacement Thought

Daily Reactions Self-Reflection

Reaction	What did you gain from reacting this way?	What needs were met?	Alternative way

Looking for Opportunities

Experience	Opportunity

Checklist:

- ☐ Meditated
- ☐ Replaced negative thoughts
- ☐ Gratitude list
- ☐ Set positive intentions
- ☐ Self-reflection
- ☐ Deserve list
- ☐ Opportunities
- ☐ Self-care

Day twenty-five: ______

Meditation

Today's meditation is a beautiful exercise in 'Expanding Awareness'. Enjoy!

My positive intentions for today are:

1. ______
2. ______
3. ______

Ten things/people/experiences I am grateful for today:

1. ______
2. ______
3. ______
4. ______
5. ______
6. ______
7. ______
8. ______
9. ______
10. ______

Replacing Negative Thoughts

Negative Thought	Cause	Replacement Thought

Daily Reactions Self-Reflection

Reaction	What did you gain from reacting this way?	What needs were met?	Alternative way

Looking for Opportunities

Experience	Opportunity

Checklist:

- ☐ Meditated
- ☐ Replaced negative thoughts
- ☐ Gratitude list
- ☐ Set positive intentions
- ☐ Self-reflection
- ☐ Deserve list
- ☐ Opportunities
- ☐ Self-care

DAY TWENTY-SIX:

Self-Care (Exercise)

Today, begin to add a little exercise into your routine. Even walking and spending time outdoors will remind you of your worth and value. Enjoy!

My positive intentions for today are:

1. ______________________________
2. ______________________________
3. ______________________________

Ten things/people/experiences I am grateful for today:

1. ______________________________
2. ______________________________
3. ______________________________
4. ______________________________
5. ______________________________
6. ______________________________
7. ______________________________
8. ______________________________
9. ______________________________
10. ______________________________

Replacing Negative Thoughts

Negative Thought	Cause	Replacement Thought

Daily Reactions Self-Reflection

Reaction	What did you gain from reacting this way?	What needs were met?	Alternative way

Looking for Opportunities

Experience	Opportunity

Checklist:

- ☐ Meditated
- ☐ Replaced negative thoughts
- ☐ Gratitude list
- ☐ Set positive intentions
- ☐ Self-reflection
- ☐ Deserve list
- ☐ Opportunities
- ☐ Self-care

Day twenty-seven:

Meditation

Today's amazing meditation is called, 'Awakening'. Enjoy!

My positive intentions for today are:

1. ____________________
2. ____________________
3. ____________________

Ten things/people/experiences I am grateful for today:

1. ____________________
2. ____________________
3. ____________________
4. ____________________
5. ____________________
6. ____________________
7. ____________________
8. ____________________
9. ____________________
10. ____________________

Replacing Negative Thoughts

Negative Thought	Cause	Replacement Thought

Daily Reactions Self-Reflection

Reaction	What did you gain from reacting this way?	What needs were met?	Alternative way

Looking for Opportunities

Experience	Opportunity

Checklist:

- ☐ Meditated
- ☐ Replaced negative thoughts
- ☐ Gratitude list
- ☐ Set positive intentions
- ☐ Self-reflection
- ☐ Deserve list
- ☐ Opportunities
- ☐ Self-care

Day twenty-eight:

Journaling

By now you are a pro at meditation. We are going to up the game now by doing some creative writing, or journaling, after your meditations. Begin by writing out what you saw and felt, and then let yourself go. Enjoy!

My positive intentions for today are:

1. ______________________________
2. ______________________________
3. ______________________________

Ten things/people/experiences I am grateful for today:

1. ______________________________
2. ______________________________
3. ______________________________
4. ______________________________
5. ______________________________
6. ______________________________
7. ______________________________
8. ______________________________
9. ______________________________
10. ______________________________

Replacing Negative Thoughts

Negative Thought	Cause	Replacement Thought

Daily Reactions Self-Reflection

Reaction	What did you gain from reacting this way?	What needs were met?	Alternative way

Looking for Opportunities

Experience	Opportunity

Checklist:

- ☐ Meditated
- ☐ Replaced negative thoughts
- ☐ Gratitude list
- ☐ Set positive intentions
- ☐ Self-reflection
- ☐ Deserve list
- ☐ Opportunities
- ☐ Self-care

Day twenty-nine:

Meditation

Today's beautiful meditation is geared towards healing your 'Inner child'. Enjoy!

My positive intentions for today are:

1. ____________________
2. ____________________
3. ____________________

Ten things/people/experiences I am grateful for today:

1. ____________________
2. ____________________
3. ____________________
4. ____________________
5. ____________________
6. ____________________
7. ____________________
8. ____________________
9. ____________________
10. ____________________

Replacing Negative Thoughts

Negative Thought	Cause	Replacement Thought

Daily Reactions Self-Reflection

Reaction	What did you gain from reacting this way?	What needs were met?	Alternative way

Looking for Opportunities

Experience	Opportunity

Checklist:

- ☐ Meditated
- ☐ Replaced negative thoughts
- ☐ Gratitude list
- ☐ Set positive intentions
- ☐ Self-reflection
- ☐ Deserve list
- ☐ Opportunities
- ☐ Self-care

Day thirty:

Meditation

It is our last day. You are about to complete your Thirty-Day Challenge with flying colours. Let us finish off with a beautiful 'Finding Purpose' meditation. Congratulations on all your hard work and enjoy!

My positive intentions for today are:

1. ______________________________
2. ______________________________
3. ______________________________

Ten things/people/experiences I am grateful for today:

1. ______________________________
2. ______________________________
3. ______________________________
4. ______________________________
5. ______________________________
6. ______________________________
7. ______________________________
8. ______________________________
9. ______________________________
10. ______________________________

Replacing Negative Thoughts

Negative Thought	Cause	Replacement Thought

Daily Reactions Self-Reflection

Reaction	What did you gain from reacting this way?	What needs were met?	Alternative way

Looking for Opportunities

Experience	Opportunity

Checklist:

- ☐ Meditated
- ☐ Replaced negative thoughts
- ☐ Gratitude list
- ☐ Set positive intentions
- ☐ Self-reflection
- ☐ Deserve list
- ☐ Opportunities
- ☐ Self-care

Survivor to Warrior

Lisa Cybaniak

This book was twenty years in the making, and only came together now thanks to the amazing support and dedication of several key people I would like to acknowledge.

First, my husband Stefan. You are the single greatest man I know. Your undying devotion to your family is inspiring. Your support in my decision to share my story, quit my job and begin a business serving others, despite all the unknowns and obvious obstacles in our path, fills my heart with joy and my soul with strength. I love you more than words can express.

No book would be complete without thanking my two stepsons, Kye and Oscar, for their patience and love while I navigate the new waters of step-motherhood. Life would be incomplete without you.

I could not possibly leave out the most important person in my life, my rock, and quite literally my saviour, my mum Shirley. The sacrifices you made over the years as a single mother are large indeed. To pick up only a few things and leave an entire life behind, not once but twice, to give me the best and save me from harm, is something only the strongest people can do. You never asked questions. You never doubted me for a second. You have always been the one constant in my life; the person who supported me while I struggled to learn how to break through the cocoon, spread my wings and become the beautiful butterfly you always knew I was. It is because of your unwavering love that I first began to see the light.

Daniella Blechner of Conscious Dreams Publishing also deserves huge praise. Danni, you are my Book Journey Mentor, but also a miracle worker when it comes to getting the best from a writer. The coaching, courses and support materials were excellent. As a knowledge-seeker, I devoured everything you had to teach me, which was a lot. I am also proud to call you my friend. The journey of publishing this first book with you has been incredible. I have felt supported and inspired every step of the way, and I cannot wait to travel this road together many more times in the future.

Jae Thompson, the genius behind my cover design, also deserves my deepest thanks. Jae, your talent screams through this cover design, but what others do not realise is the amount of patience it takes to work with a writer who begins this process with no real concept of what she wants her cover to look like. You listened to my scattered ideas and pulled out all the important details to create a masterpiece that perfectly symbolises the theme of the entire book. I am forever grateful for your efforts, patience, talent and ability to understand what your clients need.

Lee Dickinson, my editor, is meticulous with his work and quite simply the best in the business. Being my first book, Lee had his hands full. In true professional fashion, he stepped up and guided me every step of the way. Thank you, Lee, for your hard work and patience.

Thank you to Nadia Vitushynska, my typesetter, for working so diligently to ensure the essence of my message was appropriately captured.

Lastly, I would like to thank my friends and family who came forward to support me after I first shared my story of abuse and recovery. When you spend your whole life hiding your past in fear of how those around you will respond, being greeted with open arms, a shoulder and looks of admiration filled me with such warmth, acceptance and love. Your words of encouragement and support fuelled me to change my career to help others, and to finally sit down and accomplish the tremendous task of writing my book, and continue to break my silence in an effort to shed the stigma of being abused. I am honoured to have so many loving and kind people in my life, and I am grateful for each of you.

About the Author

Canadian born Lisa Cybaniak, is an Oxfordshire-based NLP coach, motivational speaker, founder of Life, like you mean it! She was inspired along this career path after fighting to heal from ten years of child abuse.

Lisa began her career as a Registered Massage Therapist, enjoying the immense feeling of helping others to heal through the power of positive touch. She quickly added several more healing modalities to her repertoire, including becoming a Reiki master, acupuncturist, doula, and Lamaze Childbirth Educator. For sixteen years, Lisa took pride in owning her own business helping people to heal physically.

By her mid-thirties, Lisa was ready to challenge herself. She became a science teacher and moved to England. Unhappy with the education system, Lisa quickly realised she needed to take action to find peace and happiness within. After meeting her husband and stepsons, she decided to continue to help people on a deeper level. She decided to pen her first blog, Life, like you mean it! which gave birth to her writing career.

With her successful blog on surviving and thriving after child abuse, she is now on a mission to shed the stigma of being abused by breaking her silence, while empowering other survivors to build the life they deserve.

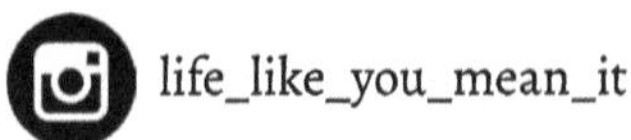

www.lifelikeyoumeanit.com

lisacybaniak@lifelikeyoumeanit.com

Be the author of your own destiny

Find out more about our authors, events, products and how, too, can get your book journey started.

Conscious Dreams Publishing

@DreamsConscious

@consciousdreamspublishing

Daniella Blechner

www.consciousdreamspublishing.com

info@consciousdreamspublishing.com

Let's connect